...DISCOVER

NOVA SCOTIA

HISTORIC SITES

ALEXA THOMPSON

Co-published by
The Province of Nova Scotia
and Nimbus Publishing Limited

Co-published by the Province of Nova Scotia
and Nimbus Publishing Limited.
Sponsored by:

Economic Development and Tourism
A product of the Nova Scotia Government Co-publishing Program

Design: Arthur Carter, Halifax
Cover Photo: Balmoral Grist Mill, courtesy of Nova Scotia Tourism
Photo Credits: On the following pages, images are courtesy of the
Nova Scotia Museum: 4, 5, 9, 10, 11, 13, 18, 20, 27, 30, 31, 54,
59, 63, 76, 85, 87, 90, 91, 92
On the following pages, images are courtesy of Nova Scotia
Tourism: 3, 6, 7, 8 (top and second from bottom), 14, 15, 16, 17,
19, 22, 23, 24, 25, 26, 28, 29, 46, 47, 48, 49, 50, 51, 53 (top), 55,
56, 57, 58, 60, 62, 64, 65, 66, 68, 69, 72, 74, 80, 84, 86, 88, 89,
93, 94, 95, 96, 97
On the following pages, images are courtesy of the museum or
historic site: 32, 52, 70, 75, 78, 79, 83
On the following page, image is courtesy of Prince of Wales
Martello Tower NHS, Parks Canada: 71

Printed and bound by Printcrafters Inc.

Canadian Cataloguing in Publication Data
Thompson, Alexa
Discover Nova Scotia, historic sites
Co-published by N.S. Dept. of Economic Development and
Tourism.
Includes index
ISBN 1-155109-254-9

1. Historic sites—Nova Scotia—Guidebooks. 2. Nova Scotia—
Guidebooks. 3. Nova Scotia—History. I. Nova Scotia. Dept. of
Economic Development and Tourism. II. Title.
FC2307.T46 1999   917.1604'4 C97-950251-9
F1037.T46 1999

Nimbus Publishing acknowledges the financial assistance of the
Canada Council and the Department of Canadian Heritage.

Contents

Introduction

Nova Scotia has a colourful past. Topography, location, wars, and famine in Europe have all helped shape the province's prehistory and history.

During the Jurassic Age, dinosaurs roamed here; fossils of some of the world's smallest and oldest dinosaurs can be found in the Parrsboro area and are on display at the Fundy Geological Museum. Six hundred million years later the region was blanketed in ice several miles thick. Glaciers gouged out valleys, leaving behind fertile land, rounded the tops of mountains, and sculpted the jagged coastline, leaving behind natural harbours that eons later attracted early European fishermen—not to mention the deep, ice-free harbour that helped to turn Halifax by the mid-1800s, into a major centre of trade and commerce.

The first people in Nova Scotia were Paleo-Indians, who arrived in the region 11,000 years ago. They survived by hunting caribou and when the herds dwindled, they moved on. Around 7,500 years ago, Maritime Archaic Indians moved into the Maritimes to fish the coastal waters, hunt sea mammals, trap small game animals, and gather roots and berries. The Mi'kmaq, who arrived about 2,500 years ago, are possibly descendants of the Maritime Archaic Indians.

Excellent craftspeople, the Mi'kmaq dyed porcupine quills and used the colourful shafts in patterns on containers and clothing—many examples of which can be viewed at the Museum of Natural History in Halifax. In summer the Mi'kmaq hugged the coastline, catching and drying fish. In winter they moved their camps inland to hunt deer, moose, and other game. Their expertise at hunting was much prized by later European explorers who traded with the Mi'kmaq for furs to sell in Europe.

Who knows who was the first European to arrive in Nova Scotia? Some say it was Prince Henry Sinclair of Scotland, who may have sailed up the Bay of Fundy in 1398 and spent a year with the Mi'kmaq. History, however, records that Italian explorer John Cabot arrived in 1497 on behalf of the King of England. He sailed around the mainland and up the coast of Cape Breton and claimed all he saw for the English king. Cabot returned with tales of his crew dipping their fingers into the sea to haul out fish. These stories excited European fishermen, many of whom over the next one hundred years started coming in the summers to fish the waters, setting up camps along the coast and trading with the Mi'kmaq—items such as blankets and tools for furs. Artifacts from this period, too, can be seen at the Museum of Natural History.

In 1534 Jacques Cartier explored the region and claimed it for France. While both England and France declared ownership of the same areas, neither country set up a permanent settlement during the sixteenth century—although the stage was set for conflict for the ensuing 150 years. But during the 1500s the French were content to concentrate on fishing off the coast of Nova Scotia, while English explorers ventured farther inland for furs.

Early in the 1600s King Henry IV of France decided it was time to take control of the English fur trade. He appointed Pierre du Gua de Monts, with his explorer and cartographer Samuel de Champlain, to set up a permanent settlement in what became known as Acadie or Acadia. The first winter in 1604 was a disaster, with half the settlers dying. But come spring, de Monts and Champlain established Canada's first viable settlement at Port Royal (Annapolis Royal), where today tourists can visit a replica of the original habitation. Although most of the first inhabitants returned home after three years—when Henry IV abandoned interest in the site—other French farmers arrived with their families, lured by stories of a rich and fertile land. Known as Acadians, they farmed in the Annapolis Valley, building dykes along the Fundy shore to stop the world's highest tides from flooding their fields. Many of these dykes are still visible, especially in the Grand Pré area, the main site of the 1755 Acadian deportation.

By the 1600s, seventy Acadian families lived in the region, receiving support from the Mi'kmaq and trading with English settlers in what are now the New England States. But both England and France wanted sole control of the lucrative fishing and fur trades in the region and were prepared to fight in order to get it. From 1604 until 1710, control of Acadia was tossed between these two countries nine times.

By 1713 the French had lost control of all of Acadia, except for Cape Breton (Île Royal) and Prince Edward Island (Île St. Jean). To defend Cape Breton they built Fortress Louisbourg, now a magnificent restored fortified town but one that, at the time, brought France to the edge of bankruptcy. England, with its fortress at the Citadel in Halifax, ruled the rest of the province and named it Nova Scotia, meaning New Scotland. Those Acadian farmers and fishermen who chose to remain under English rule (many moving to Cape Breton under French control) lived an uneasy peace under their new government.

In the mid-1700s, with war between Britain and France still raging in Europe and North America, the British became concerned about the Acadians' loyalty to the throne of England. In 1755 Charles Lawrence, British governor of Nova Scotia, demanded the Acadians swear an oath of loyalty. Those who refused were driven into exile. Over 6,000 Acadians were deported. This expulsion and the defeat of the French at Louisbourg in 1758, and at Quebec City in 1759, spelled the end of French rule in North America.

Acadian land was turned over to British settlers and to Loyalists fleeing the American Revolution of 1775-76. Although many Acadians did return after an amnesty was declared, they found their lands occupied by English-speaking settlers, and were forced to make new homes in less fertile areas, such as along the shore from Yarmouth to Digby, where many turned to fishing for a living. Many of the fine historic homes along Nova Scotia's Evangeline Trail stand on land that once belonged to the Acadians.

The end of the French/British wars heralded a time of prosperity for Nova Scotia. Thousands of immigrants arrived from New England, the British Isles (particularly Scotland and Ireland, which were ravaged by land clearances and famine), Germany, and Switzerland. People of different nationalities settled in various areas together, and brought with them their skills and the place names of their hometowns and villages. Hence, German farmers, later becoming shipbuilders, settled in Lunenburg while English fishermen put down roots in Liverpool. Among the influx of New England Loyalists were a number of Black slaves seeking freedom. There remain strong Black communities in, among other places, Halifax/Dartmouth and surrounding Shelburne on the South Shore.

By the early 1800s, immigrants arrived daily from the United States and Europe. They settled in small communities, cleared the land, and built homes, roads, schools, and churches. Most earned a living as farmers or fishermen, but many enterprising individuals set up businesses to serve their communities—stores, mills, and shipbuilding facilities in particular. Stores encouraged commerce. Mills ground flour or turned out logs for building. Ships were needed to maintain trade with Europe, for bringing in new immigrants and for fishing. During the Golden Age of Sail, shipyards stretched along the Bay of Fundy and the South Shore. By the mid-1800s, Nova Scotia had one of the largest shipping fleets in the world. Many of the world's most famous ships were built here, such as the doomed nineteenth-century *Mary Celeste*, built on Spencers Island and later found in full sail but abandoned; and the twentieth-century schooner, *Bluenose,* built in Lunenburg.

Halifax soon became a bustling seaport and thriving town. It was in this capital city that Canada first began to shake off the yoke of colonial rule. In the early 1800s the colony of Nova Scotia was ruled by a British governor who, although he took the advice of members of the Nova Scotia

Assembly, enacted all laws and made all final decisions. Men such as Nova Scotia patriot, Joseph Howe, felt that the people of the province should have a greater say in how they were governed. At such urging, Britain agreed to give its colony responsible government— a government elected by the people to create and enforce local laws. There is a statue honouring Joseph Howe outside of the legislative assembly building in Halifax.

A moonlit farmhouse along the Glooscap Trail.

With a taste for responsible government, politicians soon considered a united Canada. On July 1, 1867, the colonies of what are now Ontario, Quebec, New Brunswick, and Nova Scotia came together as the Dominion of Canada.Confederation had a strong and long-lasting effect on Nova Scotia. One of the terms of Confederation was to build the

Intercolonial Railway. Trains meant easier trade among the provinces, and towns quickly sprang up along the line. Confederation also meant the decline of the Shubenacadie Canal system, running from the Dartmouth waterfront to the Bay of Fundy. The canal had enabled ships to sail across Nova Scotia's inland waterways rather than around the coastline. The railroad also meant that immigrants could now settle farther west. In the mid-1800s Nova Scotia was the final destination of most immigrants. By the early to mid-1900s most new arrivals stepped off the boat in Halifax and onto a train taking them west. Although there are few of these passenger trains left, there are museums dedicated to the nineteenth-century glory days of the railway, such as the Antigonish Heritage Museum, the Sydney and Louisburg Railway Museum, Louisburg, and the Orangedale Railway Station Museum on Cape Breton Island.

The railway had an enormous impact on the province's economy. For one thing it meant jobs—not only to build the lines and the trains, but to power the locomotives. The engines used Nova Scotia coal for fuel, and soon mines were in operation in northern Nova Scotia and industrial Cape Breton, near Sydney. Museums in Springhill and Glace Bay remind visitors of the mining heyday in Nova Scotia—and of its inherent dangers. Steel was also in great demand for building locomotives and steamships. Samuel Cunard may have run his shipping line from what is now Historic Properties on Halifax's waterfront, but steel to build ships was forged in Sydney—a booming industrial town until the end of World War I.

The First World War was a busy time for Halifax. Already a centre for trade and shipbuilding, the city served as an international naval headquarters. It still retains its ties with the navy, as evidenced by the Maritime Command Museum. But World War I was also the scene of one of the world's worst man-made disasters. On December 6, 1917, two ships (one of which was *Mont Blanc*, loaded with munitions) collided in Halifax Harbour. *Mont Blanc* caught fire and attracted hundreds of Haligonians to the waterfront to watch the blaze. Then, at 9:05 a.m., the ship exploded, levelling the north end of Halifax and much of Dartmouth. The explosion killed 2,000 people and injured a further 8,000. This tragic event is remembered every December 6 at the memorial bells atop the hill at Fort Needham in Halifax.

The years between the wars were not particularly kind to Nova Scotia. During the Depression, thousands lost their jobs as the economy collapsed, and many moved away to seek work. But the advent of the Second World War brought a revival, especially to Halifax. Once again the docks bustled with the activity of troops as ships were loaded with soldiers and weapons, ready to set out in convoys to relieve beleaguered Great Britain.

The prosperity continued through the 1950s and well into the 1960s as the province used some of the money earned during the war years to build schools, roads, and community centres. New indus-

tries and fish processing plants sprang up around the province, promising even better times. But by the late 1970s the potential boom had gone flat. Coal was running out in Cape Breton. Fewer steel-hulled ships were built, forcing closure of many of Sydney's steel mills. A downturn in the wooden boat market spelled disaster for many small-town shipyards. And, in the 1980s, the decline in fish stocks resulted in the closure of hundreds of fish processing plants, large and small. There have been compensations, however. The pulp and paper industry grew rapidly during the 1980s, and the 1990s have been witness to the emergence of many new businesses in information technology and communications. Where once John Cabot's sailors could dip their hands into the sea and draw up fish by the barrel, and later deep-sea trawlers hauled tonnes of fish to the processing plants, today the focus is offshore gas production.

Nova Scotia has a rich and colourful past. It was here that dinosaurs roamed, and where the

An aerial view of the Halifax Citadel, a National Historic Site.

Mi'kmaq fished and hunted with the seasons. Here the first European explorers traded with the Mi'kmaq for furs, fuelling a continental desire for exotic furs; here the first permanent settlement in Canada was founded; and here the French and English fought for control of North America. Here responsible government was first established, and it was here that so many nineteenth-century writers, politicians, and businessmen and women lived, prospered, and built many of the fine historic homes dotted throughout the province. Here, too, immigrants from Europe and the United States arrived daily in the thousands, bringing a unique cultural diversity to the province, and here ship-building, mining, forestry, and fishing abounded. And it was from here that the troops sailed for Europe during World Wars I and II, and where the convoys gathered which provided the lifeline to the allied forces.

Symbols

 Washroom

 Information

 Wheelchair access

 National park/site

 Parking

 Provincial site

 Food

 Picnic Area

 Admission

Evangeline Trail

Evangeline Trail

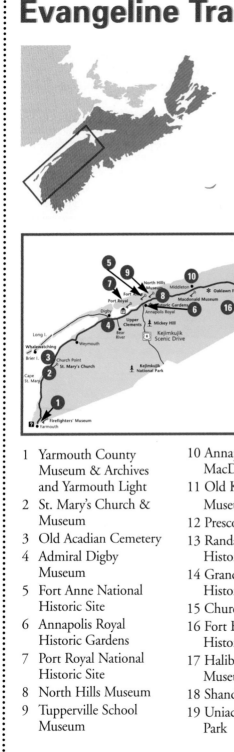

1 Yarmouth County Museum & Archives and Yarmouth Light
2 St. Mary's Church & Museum
3 Old Acadian Cemetery
4 Admiral Digby Museum
5 Fort Anne National Historic Site
6 Annapolis Royal Historic Gardens
7 Port Royal National Historic Site
8 North Hills Museum
9 Tupperville School Museum
10 Annapolis Valley MacDonald Museum
11 Old King's Courthouse Museum
12 Prescott House Museum
13 Randall House Historical Museum
14 Grand Pré National Historic Site
15 Churchill House
16 Fort Edward National Historic Site
17 Haliburton House Museum
18 Shand House Museum
19 Uniacke Estate Museum Park

Introduction

Running up the backbone of Nova Scotia, from Yarmouth along the Acadian shore to Digby and through the rich Annapolis Valley, is the Evangeline Trail. Its turbulent history is marked by years of conflict between the British and the French, followed by years of prosperity.

The first half of this trail follows the coastline explored and mapped by Samuel de Champlain in the early 1600s, and it was here at Port Royal (Annapolis Royal) that he established the first permanent European settlement north of Florida. Port Royal became not only a focal point for Acadian

The scenic Evangeline Trail.

settlers from France who arrived to farm the fertile soil of the Annapolis Valley; it also became a pawn in the French–English struggle for control of North America. In a little over one hundred years, control of the region changed hands nine times.

Grand Pré, at the eastern end of the Valley, is remembered as a debarkation point for many of the Acadians sent into exile by the British in 1755. The site is immortalized in Henry Wadsworth Longfellow's poem, *Evangeline*, to whose legendary namesake a statue has been erected at the site.

A number of Acadians returned after the Deportation, but settled along the shore from Yarmouth to Digby in a string of small villages. The many fine churches along the drive are examples of their contribution to the architecture and culture of the region. You will even find cemeteries with stones marking the graves of Acadians dating to the late seventeenth century.

Acadian farmlands were handed over to British and Loyalist settlers, who prospered, building fine homes, schools, and churches of their own. The many beautiful historic homes through the Annapolis Valley, such as Prescott House, Haliburton House, and the estate of Richard John Uniacke, were built by prosperous merchants and statesmen. The region was also an important shipping centre during the nineteenth century, a time when Hantsport was the fifth largest shipbuilding port in the world. You can discover a part of Nova Scotia's shipbuilding past in the Marine Memorial room in Churchill House, Hantsport and at Lawrence House Museum in Maitland.

Discover
Nova Scotia
Historic Sites

Yarmouth County Museum and Archives & Yarmouth Light

In 1604 the bow of Samuel de Champlain's ship made its way into the point he named Cape Forchu, and he made many friends with the area natives—the Mi'kmaq.

By 1653 European settlers had made their way to the southern tip of Nova Scotia and colonized Pubnico. The town of Yarmouth, mentioned by name in a dispatch of 1759, is considered to have been founded in 1761. It is filled with ornate houses that reflect the town's rich shipbuilding heritage, built by shipping magnates during the nineteenth century.

The award-winning Yarmouth County Museum, housed in a century-old church, reflects the seafaring past of Yarmouth. You will discover an eclectic assortment of Victorian artifacts and marine heritage. Eighty oil paintings of ships hang on the walls. On display is the original inlaid compound lens from the old Cape Forchu light (c. 1840), an 1866 stagecoach, and a turn-crank Concert Roller Organ.

Following the Cape Forchu scenic drive on Route 304 will take you to the site where the Cape Forchu light was installed. Today the Federal Heritage property contains a fisherman's monument and new lighthouse built in the 1960s. An interpretive and information centre sits on the property. The walking trails, sandy beaches, and splendid views make it well worth the extra drive.

Directions: The Yarmouth County Museum & Archives is located off Main Street, between Parade and Forest Streets, at 22 Collins Street, Yarmouth.

The Yarmouth Light is on Route 304, 11 km (7 mi.) from Yarmouth on Cape Forchu Scenic Drive.

Yarmouth County Museum & Archives:
(902) 742-5539
Open year-round
June 1-Oct 15: Mon-Sat: 9 a.m.-5 p.m.;
Sun 2-5 p.m.
Oct 16-May 31: Tues-Sat 9 a.m.-5 p.m.; Sun 2-5 p.m.
Archives: 10 a.m.-4 p.m.; Sun 2-4 p.m.

This museum features five period rooms and a research library with genealogical material on Yarmouth families.

Yarmouth Light:
(902)742-1433
Open year-round
Interpretive Centre open May 1-Oct 31

The Yarmouth Light affords a magnificent seascape view.

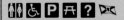

St. Mary's Church and Museum

St. Mary's Church
Museum:
(902) 769-2808
Open July 1-Oct 14:
9:30 a.m.-5:30 p.m.
Off season: by
appointment

Its towering spire
makes the church a
dramatic sight.

Some of the largest churches in rural Nova Scotia
are found strung along the Acadian shore like beads
on a rosary. Standing tall in the village of Church
Point is Église Ste. Marie (St. Mary's Church).
Designed by Augustine Regneault, Église Ste. Marie
is the most spectacular structure of its kind. With
its spire shooting upward to a height of 185 feet, it
is the highest wooden church in North America.

Regneault's castle-like design was influenced by
the famous chateaux of the Loire Valley, near his
home in Rennes, France. Under the guidance of
master carpenter, Leo Melanson, this enormous
structure rose in 1905. The giant timber frame sits
adjacent to the campus of Nova Scotia's only
French university, Université Ste. Anne, where it is
under continual siege from the bay's forceful gales.
Disaster almost hit during one such storm in
1914, when the steeple was struck by lightning
and ignited into flames. Wondrously, a burst of
rain saved the grand edifice.

Visitors are welcome to the church and its
museum, complete with period-dressed guides.
Directions: St. Mary's Church is on the shore road
about 71 km from Yarmouth, Route 1 to Church
Point, adjacent to Université Ste. Anne.

Old Acadian Cemetery

Open year-round
at all hours

The old Acadian Cemetery and "La Petite
Chapelle" lies just a short distance fromt the village
of Grosses Coques. Once an island where the
Mi'kmaq may have buried their dead, this rocky
shore was a haven for Pierre (Piau) Belliveau and
the 120 Acadians who had escaped deportation in
1755. The site became the first cemetery in Clare
Township and on September 8, 1769 the first mass
was celebrated by the missionary Abbé Bailly.

Crosses mark the first settlers in this area and
date from 1699 (Jean Beliveau) through 1755-1780
(Les Inconnus [The Unknown]). Descendants of
these pioneers are scattered throughout Clare
Township today with names like Saulnier, Guidry,
Batiste, Comeau, Gaudet, and Doucet.
Directions: Grosses Coques is the next village past
Church Point, on Route 1. Look for the sign; a dirt
road leads to the cemetery and little chapel.

Admiral Digby Museum

Famous for its scallops and "Digby Chicks" (a type of small smoked herring), the town of Digby is a main entry point to the province because it opens up to the Bay of Fundy through the Annapolis Basin and Digby Gut. The town provides ferry service to Saint John, New Brunswick. The county has a rich social and cultural fabric made up of Mi'kmaq, Acadians, British, and Black Loyalists, all of whom are represented in the Admiral Digby Museum.

Admiral Digby
Museum: (902) 245-
6322
Open June 22-Aug
31: 9 a.m.-5 p.m.
Sept: 1-4 p.m.
Off season: by
appointment

The Georgian-style house is named after Admiral Robert Digby. It was under Digby that New England Loyalists, who arrived by ship in 1783, first colonized the area.

Not far from the municipal visitor information centre, the home is open to the public. No rooms are roped off; you may enter into each and experience the parlour, kitchen, bedroom, a seafaring heritage collection, and a series of watercolours of Sable Island (c. 1834) by J. Gilpin. Look for the child's nursery, Mi'kmaq woven baskets, nineteenth-century costumes, art exhibits, and period photographs. Genealogical resources are available.

The elegant ethos of the Georgian period as well as Digby's sea-faring past are brought to life in the museum's many displays.

The museum also plays host to a wealth of information and fun facts about scallops, the industry that makes Digby famous today.

Directions: The museum is situated in downtown Digby, at 95 Montague Row.

Fort Anne:
(902) 532-2397
Open year-round
Building: Open
May 15-Oct 15:
9 a.m.-6 p.m.
Off season: by
chance or
appointment

Once humming with commerce and shipping, this historic community of six hundred now relies on tourism as its main trade. During much of the early eighteenth century Annapolis Royal was the seat for the government of Nova Scotia, and therefore played a key role in the early history of Canada under both French and British regimes. In a little cemetery near Fort Anne, some of the oldest tombstones and grave markers in Canada are found.

In 1702 the original Fort Anne earthworks were built in the French Vauban style—named after the seventeenth-century military engineer Marshall Vauban. The works had sloping walls and projecting bastions to counter artillery fire. A 30-foot-wide protected parapet once lined the perimeter of the deep ditch, allowing space for reinforcements to move in times of siege. The oldest remaining French structure is a gunpowder magazine. After the British took control it was sometimes used as a prison.

The first fort was built here c.1629.

Archeological work is being done under the closely cropped lawns of the Fort to uncover the foundations of the building where Governor Jean Paul Mascarene worked and lived. Mascarene was a French Huguenot military officer who served in the British Army from 1710 to 1740.

From the flagpole of the main building hangs a replica of the original Great Union flag of Britain, which dates from 1606 to 1801. Inside the building is the Fort Anne Heritage tapestry, designed by Kiyoko Grenier Saso and crafted by one hundred volunteers, using three million stitches. Its colourful panels depict the Fort's four centuries of history: Port Royal, Annapolis Royal, Fort Anne, and the National Park of today.

A painting of the town of Annapolis Royal.

Directions: The site is in the town of Annapolis Royal. Take Exit 22 off Highway 101 and continue north on Route 8. Proceed through the traffic lights on Upper Saint George Street and take the second left into Fort Anne.

 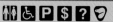

Annapolis Royal Historic Gardens

A garden for every season, towering trees, and blossoming shrubs weave together four centuries of history in the Annapolis Royal Historic Gardens. Inquiring and contemplative minds will find pleasure amidst the fragrance and vibrant colour of these exotic gardens.

Annapolis Royal
Historic Gardens:
(902) 532-7018
Open mid-May–mid-
Oct: 8 a.m.–dusk

The ten-acre grounds of the Historic Gardens contain almost a dozen different gardens, all beautiful and unique in their own right. The Rose Garden, which includes a Rose Maze, boasts approximately two thousand rose bushes. The Hybrid Tea Rose is of particular beauty, as is the vivid Forest Fire. The quiet ponds and interesting rock plinths are enhanced by the heavenly perfume of the huge Castor Bean plant.

A replica of an Acadian Cottage—reminiscent of a simpler life—with a "potager," sits on the grounds of the Historic Gardens and welcomes visitors to linger. This traditional French-style vegetable garden has wide paths dividing four symmetrical plots.

Garden lovers will
find plenty of
attractions here.

The Marsh Look-off reveals a panorama of reclaimed salt marsh, still one of Nova Scotia's best agricultural areas. Here, tall spears of green grasses with burnt-brown tassels wave in the wind. It is likely that the first North American dykes were hand-constructed on this very spot by Acadians, perhaps in the late 1600s. The Historic Gardens are open May through October to strollers, garden lovers, artists, poets, historians, and anyone else who loves colour or the tenderness of growing things.

Direction: Same as reaching Fort Anne (see page 6), but situated further along at 441 Upper Saint George Street, a short walk.

The Gardens are the centrepiece of this historically rich town.

Port Royal National Historic Park

Port Royal:
(902) 532-2898
Open daily
May 15-Oct 15:
Mon-Sat 9 a.m.-6 p.m.;
Sun 9 a.m.-5:30 p.m.

With game, wooded hills, wide rivers, and towering cliffs encircling a bay that would hold "a thousand vessels," Samuel de Champlain found the perfect spot for a habitation and fort in 1605. Considered one of the first European settlements in North America, the site was called Port Royal.

Now a National Historic Park, the Port Royal Habitation is a fascinating replica of the original fur trading post built by Champlain and his superior,

Sieur de Monts.

The Habitation was home to Canada's first theatrical performance.

Sieur de Monts. The rectangular wooden structure is built around a courtyard, similar to farms in Normandy, France. The interior of the main building is so well-staged that each room, or dwelling, breathes history. In the gentlemen's dwelling, wide-brimmed felt hats hang on wooden pegs next to the curtained double bunks near the fireplace. And in the common room, furs are thrown over chairbacks as though members of the colony has just burst in to settle down to the Order of Good Cheer—a social club designed to alleviate the boredom of dreary winters. There is also a forge, kitchen, bakery room and ovens, and the artisans' quarters. Upstairs is a sealed-off sick bay, more gentlemen's quarters, and Sieur de Monts' private dwelling.

Guides dressed in period costume navigate the extensive grounds, giving visitors a vivid sense of the accomplishments of these early settlers.

Directions: The site is located west of Granville Ferry and Annapolis Royal on Route 8. Turn right onto Route 1 at the traffic lights. Cross the causeway and take the first left following the signs to Port Royal, about 10.5 km (6.5 mi.).

Samuel de Champlain.

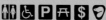

North Hills Museum

This old framed house, filled with elegant furnishings and antiques, has a history of many owners. Overlooking the Annapolis Basin, and across the causeway from Annapolis Royal, the cosy dwelling was an Acadian farm before land grants were given to Loyalist settlers in 1764. It was known as Rumsey Farm until the early 1800s, and then as Amberman House until Robert Patterson, an antiques dealer and banker, bought the house in 1969 and renamed it North Hills. He lived here among his collection of eighteenth-century paintings, English porcelain and glassware, and many other antiques.

North Hills Museum: (902) 532-2168 Open June 1-Oct 15: Mon-Sat 9:30 a.m.- 5:30 p.m.; Sun 1-5:30 p.m.

Inside, notice the Georgian decor created by Patterson as well as a Jacobean piece of furniture (c. 1660) with oak drawers and metal locks. The exposed wooden beams, ladder to the loft, double flute chimney, original masonry, and guest bedroom add great charm to this simple historic dwelling, which Patterson bequeathed to the province in 1974.

Directions: Enter Annapolis Royal on Route 8, turn right onto Route 1 at the traffic lights. Cross the causeway and take the first left. North Hills Museum is only a few kilometres along Route 1.

The North Hills Museum contains an impressive assortment of Georgian furniture, paintings, glassware, and ceramics.

9 Tupperville School Museum

Tupperville School
Museum: (902) 665-
2579
Open mid-May-
Labour Day:
10 a.m.-6 p.m.

With the Annapolis River gleaming in the distance, and small farms and orchards gracing each turn, Route 201 is one of the most scenic drives in the province. About fifteen minutes southeast of Annapolis Royal is the one-room Tupperville schoolhouse, which is now open to the public as a museum.

The little red schoolhouse was built before 1875 and held classes until 1950. With artifacts including school slates, Royal Reader schoolbooks atop old pine desks, a teacher's desk and chair, a small organ, and photographs lining the walls, the Tupperville School Museum is an authentic nineteenth-century experience. Outside are a playground, running brook, tall trees, a school yard hand pump and an outhouse.

Enjoy a look at a
nineteenth-century
schoolhouse or take
in the old fashioned
ice cream festival
held here on the last
Saturday of July.

Not far down Route 201 is Bloody Creek, named for the combats between the British garrisons of Annapolis Royal and the allied French and Mi'kmaq for possession of Acadia in 1711 and 1757. A stone cairn with a plaque commemorates the bloody battles.

Directions: The Tupperville Museum is on Route 201, 16 km (10 mi.) southeast of Annapolis Royal.

Annapolis Valley Macdonald Museum

Clocks, canoes, and country stores have at least one thing in common: you can catch a glimpse of their history at the Annapolis Valley Macdonald Museum in Middleton.

Mechanical timepieces have partitioned our days for over five hundred years, and in less than sixty minutes visitors can tick through the history of clockmaking, with the most astounding collection of clocks in the Maritimes. There are grandfather clocks, Eli Terry clocks (c. 1809), looking glass clocks, ogee clocks, steeple clocks, drop clocks, and portable clocks and watches from many parts of the world. A full wall display illustrates how mechanical clocks work, and there is a replica of a clockmaker's repair shop.

Macdonald Museum:
(902) 825-6116
Open year-round
May 15-Oct 14: Mon-Sat 9 a.m.-5 p.m. Sun 1 p.m.-5 p.m. Oct 15-May 15: Mon-Fri 10:30 a.m.-5 p.m.
Off season: Mon-Fri 10:30 a.m.-5 p.m.

Canoe lovers will discover a special room dedicated to Nova Scotian canoe maker Harold Gates.

The first original Gates canoe built in 1935 is here, along with his reproductions of the Morris and Rushton designs, and Mi'kmaq traditional birchbark canoes.

Other attractions in this eclectic museum include a natural history display under a glass roof, a replica of a 1930s country store, and a turn-of-the-century classroom. Educator Sir Wilson Macdonald had this school—the first consolidated school of its kind to be established in Canada—built in 1903.

An eclectic mix of artifacts from birchbark canoes to antique clocks are found at the Macdonald Museum.

Directions: The Macdonald School building is at 21 School Street, near downtown Middleton.

Old King's Courthouse Museum

Old King's
Courthouse Museum:
(902) 678-6237
Open Sept-June:
Tues-Fri 9:30 a.m.-
4:30 p.m.
July-Aug: Mon-Fri
9:30 a.m.-4:30 p.m.;
Sat 11:30 a.m.-
4:30 p.m.

Kentville, the "shiretown" of King's County—a rural area with its own elected council—was settled in the 1760s by New England Planters who inherited the rich fertile farmlands originally developed by deported Acadians.

The turn-of-the-century Courthouse Museum in downtown Kentville is a reddish brick building that was the seat of justice and municipal government from 1903 to 1980. Today it is open to visitors so they can discover a collection of social and natural history artifacts that reflect the county. Look for the fine bird collection from the eminent ornithologist, Dr. Robie Tufts. There is also a rock and fossil exhibit, a Victorian parlour, and various

The history of the New England Planters is made accessible by a variety of interactive displays and exhibits inside the museum.

Mi'kmaq artifacts.

The national commemorative exhibit of the New England Planters includes a film and a series of hands-on exhibits for young people. In the camouflage of the simulated oak grain on the walls of the refurbished courtroom, see if you can find sketched animals that include a bear, goat, fish, and rabbit. Family genealogies, King's County cemetery records, and New England Planter materials are all found in the Courthouse basement.

Directions: Follow Route 1 from Middleton. The Old King's Courthouse Museum is at 37 Cornwallis Street in downtown Kentville.

Prescott House Museum

Nova Scotian Charles Ramage Prescott named his house "Acacia Grove" for the acacia trees which surrounded it. A successful merchant and famous horticulturist, Prescott introduced superior varieties of apples to the area and helped to establish the Fruit Grower's Association. Prescott's acacia trees were cut down years after he died, but his house—a striking example of Georgian-style architecture—still looks handsome in its setting.

The dwelling, built c. 1814, is constructed of local bricks on a rubble masonry foundation. The unique, slightly bell cast roof is dominated by four dormers and two enormous chimneys, where smoke from no fewer than seven fireplaces once rose.

As you enter on the first floor, a wide double hallway leads to large furnished rooms in each corner of the house. Four family bedrooms are upstairs, with the servants' quarters in the attic. Look for some interesting architectural details: most inside doors have six panels, some of them decorated with small, half-circle mouldings called astragals. The elegant library adds to the uniqueness of this historic house.

The elegant gardens features flowers, hedges, gardens, a sundial, stone paths, benches, picnic tables, and a peaceful and relaxing setting. Prescott introduced and developed many varieties of apples to Nova Scotia—most notably, the Gravenstein—and was generous in providing grafting stock to Annapolis Valley farmers. An orchard established recently on the grounds will eventually bear the many varieties of apples available in Prescott's time.

In the late 1930s his great-granddaughter, Mary Allison Prescott, bought the dwelling. After the restoration in 1942 she took up residence with her two sisters. She added her collection of early needlework samplers and what is now considered one of the finest collections of tribal oriental carpets in Canada. Her wish that the house should be preserved for history has been honoured; it was designated as a National and Provincial Historic Site and is now part of the Nova Scotia Museum family.

Directions: The Prescott House Museum is off Route 358, near Wolfville, at 1633 Starr's Point Rd.

Prescott House:
(902)542-3984
Open June 1-Oct 15:
Mon-Sat 9:30 a.m.-
5:30 p.m.; Sun 1:00-
5:30 p.m.

This grandiose home and its gardens will impress you with the intricate architectural details and spacious grounds.

Prescott House sits among the most fertile farmland in the Annapolis Valley.

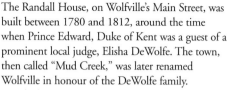

The Randall House, on Wolfville's Main Street, was built between 1780 and 1812, around the time when Prince Edward, Duke of Kent was a guest of a prominent local judge, Elisha DeWolfe. The town, then called "Mud Creek," was later renamed Wolfville in honour of the DeWolfe family.

Randall House:
(902)542-3984; off
season 684-3876
Open June 15-Sept
15: Mon-Sat 10 a.m.-
5 p.m.; Sun 2-5 p.m.

The house was owned by the Randall family until the 1920s when it fell into disrepair. In 1927 the Patriquin family bought and restored it, revitalizing the property.

Inside the house is a pleasant museum, with artifacts dating from the 1760s to the twentieth century, including New Haven clocks, a ship's organ, and Penny-Farthing bicycle from the 1890s. There are furnished bedrooms, fireplaces, a sewing room, a

At Randall House you can view a wonderful collection of locally made furniture which dates from the late seventeenth century.

large collection of ship photographs, and a dump-cart saddle on the back porch.

While visiting the Randall House, take some time in the town of Wolfville—a glorious place for walking on the nearby Acadian dykelands, with a spectacular view of the red cliffs of Blomidon.

Directions: Randall House is in downtown Wolfville at 171 Main Street.

Grand Pré National Historic Site

Passionate and inflammatory, Henry Wadsworth Longfellow's epic poem *Evangeline* still strikes a chord with people today. As visitors meander along the lush grounds of Grand Pré National Historic Site just outside Wolfville, they are drawn by the legendary Evangeline, and can better appreciate the circumstances that brought about the expulsion of more than six thousand Acadians.

Settled in 1680, Grand Pré—now dubbed the "Land of Evangeline"—was once the heart of Acadia, outgrowing Port Royal to become the largest Acadian community around the Bay of Fundy. But by the late 1800s all that remained of Grand Pré—French for "great meadow"—were the fertile dykelands and shimmering rows of willow trees.

Today as you follow the park's main paths that cross the manicured lawns you are welcomed by these ancient willow trees standing vigil beside the dykelands' look-off, not far from the red-stone, Norman-style church. Inside this historic church, which stands on the site of the original Acadian parish of Saint-Charles-des-Mines, look for artist Terry Smith-Lamothe's magnificent stained glass window depicting the expulsion.

Along one of the paths is a cross, erected in 1909 using stones from what may have been the original Acadian foundations. And of course, the grand statue of Evangeline—the work of father-son sculptors, Phillippe and Henri Hébert—stands nearby on a grassy slope, in memorial to a proud and peaceful nation.

Grand Pré:
(902) 542-3631
Open year-round

Henry Wadsworth Longfellow

Inside the stone church is a series of paintings depicting Acadian life and the Deportation.

Directions: The site is near Wolfville. From Highway 101, take Exit 10 to Wolfville and drive west on Route 1 for 1 km (0.6 mi.), and then north along the Grande Pré Road for 1 km (0.6 mi.).

Churchill House

Churchill House:
(902) 684-3365
Open summer
months: 9 a.m.-5 p.m.
(subject to change)
Off season: tours by
appointment

Situated on the Avon River, Hantsport was once the fifth largest shipbuilding port in the world. It is here that Black Nova Scotian William N. Hall (1829-1904) lived to become the first Canadian sailor and Nova Scotian to win the Victoria Cross for Valour; Hall fought in the Crimean War.

Senator Ezra Churchill, owner of Churchill and Sons Shipyards, built this attractive Victorian dwelling in 1860. Notice the stained glass windows and especially the widow's walk typical of so many coastal homes. It was on these widow's walks that wives reputedly paced while awaiting the return of their seafaring husbands, many of whom never came home.

Churchill House commemorates Hantsport's past as the fifth largest shipbuilding port in the world.

The Marine Memorial Room displays Hantsport's shipbuilding past. Artifacts include a hand-operated foghorn, masthead light, and ship's tools under glass. There are no furnishings in the main rooms, but the elegantly decorated walls and ceilings (c. 1890) were beautifully rendered by George Lyons, a local painter.

Each second-floor room is restored to its original colour and design scheme. What was once the carriage house is now a recreation building. The grounds are also used for recreational purposes, and the Nova Scotia Tourist Bureau is at the end of the driveway.

Directions: From Highway 101, take exit 8 to Hantsport. Churchill House is on Main Street, just past the town's recreation park.

Fort Edward National Historic Site

Governor Charles Lawrence, in his 1755 directive to the British soldiers charged with deporting the Acadians in the Piziquid area, is quoted as saying: "You have my orders to take an eye for an eye, a tooth for a tooth, and a life for a life." Thus the Acadian homeland was forfeited to the Crown. It was Captain Murray and Colonel Winslow who carried out the details of Lawrence's orders. Uneasy with the Acadians' refusal to take an oath of allegiance to Britain, and with constant harassment from Mi'kmaq raids, Lawrence had Fort Edward built at Windsor in 1750.

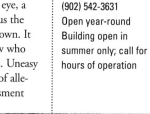

Fort Edward National Historic Site:
(902) 542-3631
Open year-round
Building open in summer only; call for hours of operation

Acadian men were taken to the Fort and later marched to the embarkation point, where with their families they were herded into the holds of vessels too small for their numbers. Carried down the Minas Basin, the Acadians sailed out of sight of their homeland.

Fort Edward is the last blockhouse still standing in Nova Scotia and the oldest of its kind in Canada.

Inside the oldest surviving blockhouse of this historic site, look for the small portholes through which four-pounder guns could be fired, and for the slit-like openings called loopholes, which were designed for rifle fire.

Interpretive markers dot the grounds explaining the locations of the original provision stores, magazine, kitchen and brewhouse, and soldiers' barracks.

During World War I, quarantine was established in the officers' quarters for the Allied Expeditionary Forces, who were camped here waiting for a convoy overseas. The small museum houses a model of the blockhouse, First World War artifacts, surveyor's chains, and mud ox shoes—to name a few rarities.

Directions: At Windsor, take Exit 6 off Highway 101. Take first left to King St., left again up Fort Edward Street.

♿ (w/assistance) P ♿

Haliburton House:
(902) 798-2915; Fax
798-5619
Open June 1-Oct 15:
Mon-Sat 9:30 a.m.-
5:30 p.m.; Sun 1-5:30
p.m.

Judge Thomas Chandler Haliburton, author of *The Clockmaker*, built this dwelling in 1836. It was Haliburton's fictional character Sam Slick, the wily Yankee peddler, who coined such sayings as "as quick as a wink," "barking up the wrong tree," and "raining cats and dogs," which are still common phrases.

Haliburton—historian, member of the Nova Scotia Legislative Assembly, and later of the British House of Commons, and a figure of national historic significance—was the first Canadian writer to win international fame for his books.

He called his estate "Clifton," and lived here with his wife Louisa, five daughters, and two sons. Built in 1836, the small but elegant one-and-a-half-storey wooden villa is shaded by maples, hemlocks, and tall elms. The house is decorated in mid-Victorian style with furnishings from Nova Scotian donors.

His creation of the character Sam Slick in *The Clockmaker*, enshrined Haliburton's reputation as a Canadian literary icon.

Notice the gilded harp in the front room and the large, handsome mirrors imported from Europe in the dining room, where part of the Weldon collection of Loyalist china is displayed. The kitchen has a cooking fireplace with a special area to keep kettles, pans, and hot irons. Upstairs are the children's rooms and master bedroom, featuring Haliburton's writing desk and an impressive antique bed from the family home of General James Wolfe.

Now part of the Nova Scotia Museum family, the house has been altered somewhat since Haliburton's time; most notable are the skylights in some of the rooms. The 29-acre estate overlooks the town of Windsor and once was enhanced by attractive fruit and flower gardens created by Mrs. Haliburton. A walking trail traverses the grounds.

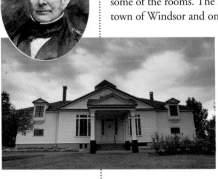

Directions: Exit 6 to Windsor, off Highway 101. The house is at 414 Clifton Avenue.

Shand House

Clifford Shand and his bride, Henrie, moved into this three-storey house especially built for them in 1890-91. Windsor was a prosperous town in the 1890s due to its excellent port during a busy era of shipping. The Shand House is particularly reflective of this prosperity. Notice the ornate woodwork, the verandahs, and the tall square tower. Clifford's father, Andrew, was a founder of the successful Windsor Furniture Factory, and several made-to-order pieces grace the house.

Shand House:
(902) 798-8213
Open June 1-Oct 15:
Mon-Sat 9:30 a.m.-
5:30 p.m.; Sun 1-5:30
p.m.

The wood trim and panelling throughout the dwelling is exceptional; the reception hall and staircases leading to the attic are made of cherry wood. Oil paintings by Henrie hang in the oak-finished dining room. Upstairs, look for the old-fashioned bathtub and dark wood panelling that give the bathroom a Victorian elegance. The children's room displays an ornamental baby carriage, crib, and toys. The master bedroom is panelled in oak and bird's-eye maple. In the attic are trunks, jars, and signs, including one that reads: "Shand's Bicycles Repaired, Windsor."

Mount the steep stairs that lead to the tower room. From here there is a beautiful view of the Minas Basin from the four windows. Clifford Shand was a cycling champion, and the photographs that line the tower walls take you back to Shand's era and his bicycling life.

Shand House sits high atop this hill overlooking Windsor.

Directions: The museum is off Route 101, in Windsor, at 389 Avon Street.

This was the first home in the province to feature indoor plumbing, central heating and gas lighting.

Uniacke Estate Museum Park

Uniacke Estate Museum Park:
(902) 866-0032
Open June 1-Oct 15:
Mon-Sat 9:30 a.m.-
5:30 p.m.; Sun 11 a.m.-
5:30 p.m.
Trails open year-
round

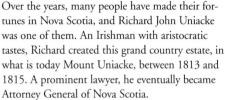

Over the years, many people have made their for-
tunes in Nova Scotia, and Richard John Uniacke
was one of them. An Irishman with aristocratic
tastes, Richard created this grand country estate, in
what is today Mount Uniacke, between 1813 and
1815. A prominent lawyer, he eventually became
Attorney General of Nova Scotia.

Note how splendidly the interior of the house
is presented. Each room is unique and filled with
excellent original Georgian furnishings. Look for
Richard's personal armchair and desk in his fine
eclectic library, which remains intact. In the base-
ment-kitchen there is now a tea room. Sumptuous
dinner parties were held in the elegant dining
room, and there are still place-settings for eight laid
at the long polished table. Upstairs are four-poster
beds, dressers, and washstands. Outside, near the
main house, are the
carriage house, the
harness room, and
grain barn.

English oaks and
cedars shade Uniacke
House, making it a
romantic place to
visit. It is one of
Canada's finest exam-
ples of the neo-
classical style of
colonial architecture, and is lovingly looked after as
part of the Nova Scotia Museum family. There are
seven walks on the property featuring forest stands,
streams, lakes, and mossy bog or a drumlin field.

At one time Uniacke's
property spanned
11,800 acres complete
with carriage house,
barn, and ice house.

Directions: From
Highway 101, take
Exit 3 to Mount
Uniacke. Then follow
the signs.

Glooscap Trail

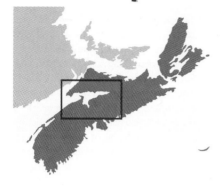

Glooscap Trail

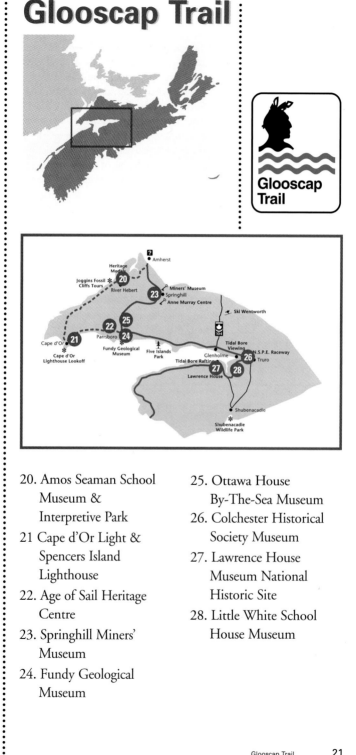

20. Amos Seaman School Museum & Interpretive Park
21. Cape d'Or Light & Spencers Island Lighthouse
22. Age of Sail Heritage Centre
23. Springhill Miners' Museum
24. Fundy Geological Museum
25. Ottawa House By-The-Sea Museum
26. Colchester Historical Society Museum
27. Lawrence House Museum National Historic Site
28. Little White School House Museum

Introduction

The Glooscap Trail along the Minas Basin takes you through an important nineteenth- and early twentieth-century industrial centre. Most who have lived here have been influenced by the sea. You will find Spencers Island, where the ill-fated *Mary Celeste* was built, and nearby Cape d'Or lighthouse, so named because Champlain thought he had discovered copper here. There are museums devoted to shipbuilding and the age of sail, and homes owned by shipbuilders and sea captains alike—all testament to the importance of trade during Nova Scotia's Golden Age of Sail. But the industrial age was also fuelled by a need for coal supplied by the mine at Springhill. With guided tours by former miners, the museum will enlighten you to the hardships endured by those who mined the coal that kept the locomotives running and the steamships afloat—all in the name of commerce.

The Glooscap Trail offers visitors a wealth of opportunities to explore the province's industrial past.

Those who wish to can also take a giant step back in time. The Fundy Geological Museum houses rocks and fossils dating to the Jurassic period when Nova Scotia was a tiny part of the single continent of Pangea.

Amos Seaman School Museum & Interpretive Park

An enterprising agriculturist, trader, ship owner, and merchant, Amos Peck "King" Seaman operated and controlled the Maritime grindstone trade in the latter half of the nineteenth century. It was in Minudie—a name derived from the Mi'kmaq word, Menoodek, which means "small bay"—that sandstone was procured to cut into grindstones. Thousands of tons of these huge grindstones, called waterstones, were quarried and exported worldwide from Minudie. Amos also established the first steam mill in Nova Scotia.

At River Head, he built the two churches and the one-room schoolhouse, which is now a restored museum dedicated to him. Photographs and documents commemorate Seaman's outstanding life and trace his genealogy.

If you look across the road, you see the main house, the once large and lavish estate where Seaman's descendants now live. It's not open to the public, but plaques displayed in the museum describe the house with its four great rooms downstairs and five bedrooms upstairs. Equipped with eight fireplaces, the house had quarters for six servants above the kitchen.

Amos Seaman School and Museum: Open July-Sept: daily 10 a.m.-6 p.m.

Museum visitors can also have a walking tour of the area.

Directions: The school museum and interpretive park are located off Route 242, at River Hebert. Turn right just past the bridge, 10 km (6 mi.).

Glooscap Trail

Cape d'Or Lighthouse & Spencers Island Lighthouse Museum

These two lighthouses offer an interesting look at the shipbuilding and natural history of the area. Here too is archaeological evidence of Paleo-Indians. The smaller of the two lighthouses, Spencers Island lighthouse, is located on Spencers Beach near the charming seaside village. The lighthouse interior houses a mini-museum of artifacts, with a photographic display of ships launched along the Parrsboro Shore.

Lighthouse &
Museum
(902) 670-0534
Cape d'Or is open
year-round.
Interpretive Centre
is seasonal.
Spencers Island
Lighthouse open
seasonally: Tues-Sun
11 a.m.-5 p.m.

The most famous vessel of them all, *Mary Celeste*, was launched from Spencers Beach in 1861. The brigantine, originally christened *Amazon*, went ashore on Cape Breton and suffered severed damage. It was salvaged by its American owners, rebuilt, and renamed *Mary Celeste*. On a voyage off the Azores in 1872, the brigantine was found without a soul aboard; Captain Benjamin Spooner Briggs, his young family, and crew of seven had all mysteriously disappeared. The strange story of this ill-fated ship has entered the annals of seafaring folklore, making *Mary Celeste* one of the most celebrated ships in sailing lore.

A panoramic view of Spencers Island.

Just a few kilometres away, perched high on a ledge above the point where the Bay of Fundy runs in to the Minas Channel, is the Cape d'Or automated lighthouse. Visitors can park at the beginning of the short road to the former lightkeepers' homes which have been converted into an interpretive centre, restaurant, and guesthouse.

A plaque commemorating the "world's most famous mystery ship," *Mary Celeste*.

The area is recognized as an International Biological Program Site. The unique habitat is the result of a distinct local climate combined with exposure to the high Fundy tides. Indian wooden tool fragments found at a nearby site have been radiocarbon dated to about two thousand years ago, about five hundred years after the Mi'kmaq arrived in the area. History and nature make this a very interesting place.

Directions: Cape d'Or is near Advocate Harbour, about 6 km (4 mi.) off Highway 209. Spencers Island is on the mainland about 6 km (4 mi.) east of Cape d'Or; look for road signs indicating Spencers Beach.

Age of Sail Heritage Centre

European farmers who came to Minas Basin in the nineteenth century soon became noted for their shipbuilding skills. "Wooden ships and iron men" is an apt description of the Parrsboro Shore, with its lumbermen, sawmills, timber merchants, and shipyards.

This rich heritage is depicted admirably in the main pavilion of the Age of Sail Heritage Centre—an old Methodist church built in 1857. The exhibits will appeal to all ages and are interspersed with mounted "poems" about the sea and the sailors.

Some of the highlights inside the museum include a photograph of the original Red House landing site and sawmill, a display of the uses of different hard and soft-woods in shipbuilding, a large binder illustrating the stages of building a wooden sailing vessel, and a small model of a Scottish galley—thought to be the type built by Henry Sinclair in Advocate Harbour in 1398-99. In the upstairs loft you can find information about the mystery of *Mary Celeste*. Other features are shipsmith's artifacts, shipbuilding tools, and ropes and pulleys.

Outside, on the surrounding grounds, look for the "Elderkin" chain, which held 7,000 logs together to form a huge raft. Thousands of sailing ships were constructed all along the coast here in the nine-teenth century, and the Centre has documented the names of the ships, their builders, and the har-bours in which they were built and launched. As you sit on the tea-house deck, you overlook the spot where ships were constructed, and the Port Greville lighthouse recently returned to its community.

Directions: The Age of Sail Heritage Centre is located on Route 209, approximately 21 km (11 mi.) west of Parrsboro.

Age of Sail Heritage Centre:
(902) 348-2060; off season 348-2030
Open May 19-Sept 1:
Tues-Sun
10 a.m.-6 p.m.
Weekends & special tours until Oct 15

Here you are welcomed into a country kitchen.

The look-off at Port Grenville.

Visit the blacksmith shop or see the original Port Greville lighthouse.

23   # Springhill Miners' Museum

Springhill Miners'
Museum:
(902) 597-8614
Open May 17-Oct 13:
Daily 9 a.m.-5 p.m.

The Springhill mine opened in the late nineteenth century in response to a need for coal. What makes this museum particularly interesting is that all the tour guides are miners or ex-miners.

Four historic events in the mine make chilling drama: 125 lives were lost in the 1891 disaster; in 1916 a subterranean fire raged through the galleries; 39 men died in the 1956 explosion; and 75 men were trapped two miles underground in the 1958 "bump."

Inside the museum there are many photographs on display, especially of the 1956 and 1958 disasters. You can see artifacts such as comfo-respirators, detonating equipment, nail boots from the 1920s, an array of safety lamps, an early signal system used underground, and coal samples.

There is also information on the first coal miners' trade union in Canada formed here at Springhill. It was called the Albion Mines Union

Association and was incorporated in 1864. Look for the original Carnegie Hero Fund Commission Gold Medal awarded to officials, workers, and local doctors who risked their lives in an attempt to rescue 174 miners in the 1958 disaster.

At the Springhill Miners' Museum, the history and the process of mining are explained.

At one point during the guided tour all the lights go out, and in that deep tunnel you get a sense of the experience of trapped miners. But the lights come back on and you have a chance to chip a piece off the tunnel wall to take home with you. On display outside is a huge coal clinker and a miners' washhouse, where all clothing and gear are hoisted up to the ceiling by ropes and pulleys. In the Lamp Cabin are miners' hats, yellow slickers, rubber boots, lamps, and a line of small boxcars on tracks.

Directions: The Springhill Miners' Museum is off Route 2 from Amherst. From Highway 104, take Exit 5 to reach Springhill. The museum is at 125 Black River Road.

Fundy Geological Museum

Along the Fundy Shore, the rusty red eroded by cliffs by the world's highest tides reveal evidence of 325-million-year-old fossils. Full of rich mineral deposits, the Fundy region is an exciting haven for rock hounds, geologists, and paleontologists.

At Five Islands Provincial Park, rare dinosaur footprints have been found in Jurassic sediments below the park, and agate occurs on Moose Island. There are zeolites in the North Mountain basalt of Partridge Island and carboniferous fossil trees at Joggins.

The museum houses impressive models offering a view of the prehistoric landscape, with life-sized models of prehistoric creatures. Roam around and view amethysts, zeolites, and agates that flash and glitter from behind glass. There are special tours of the area's beaches so that you can "walk where the dinosaurs once roamed." The Nova Scotia Gem and Mineral Show is held in Parrsboro annually, during the third week of August.

Directions: Follow Route 2 from Truro along the Bay of Fundy for about forty minutes to Parrsboro. From the NS/NB border, take Exit 104 at Amherst, follow Route 2 south for forty-five minutes. The Fundy Geological Museum is at 162 Two Islands Road. Admission charged.

Fundy Geological Museum:
(902) 254-3814
June 1-Oct 15: Daily 9:30 a.m.-5:30 p.m.
Oct 16-May 31: Tues-Sat 9 a.m.-5 p.m.;
Sun and holidays: 1-5 p.m.

Here you can discover millions of years of the province's geological history.

Ottawa House By-The-Sea Museum

Ottawa House By-The-Sea Museum: (902) 254-2376 Open June 1-September daily 10 a.m.–6 p.m. May and October by request

Sir Charles Tupper, a former prime minister of Canada, was so taken by the beauty of this Georgian-influenced oceanfront house on the red cliffs that he bought it in 1871.

One of the Fathers of Confederation, Tupper called his summer dwelling, "Ottawa House By-The-Sea." Here Sir Charles and Lady Tupper played host to many guests, most of whom were high-profile politicians. From 1924 to 1974, under a string of various owners—including an alleged bootlegger in the 1920s named Captain Carl B. Merriam—the building did very well as a thriving country inn.

Now a museum that houses artifacts and furnishings from Tupper's time, there are exhibits of seafaring, lumbering, and the social history of the Parrsboro shore. Among the Victorian furnishings in the front room is a small foot-operated bellows organ. Upstairs are the separate bedrooms of Lady Tupper and Sir Charles, along with a Victorian dressing room and sewing room. Other attractions include a marine

This property was the site for gatherings of Canada's most senior politicians.

room with a wall display of sailor's knots, a tool room and schoolroom, reflecting an area rich in history. Outside, look for the interpretive signs that describe Partridge Island, which the Mi'kmaq believe to be the home of their mythical hero, Glooscap. Champlain gathered amethysts from the island shore in the early 1600s, Acadians settled here not long afterwards, and after the 1755 Acadian expulsion, New England Planters and United Empire Loyalists arrived. The view of Cape Blomidon and the Minas Basin is breathtaking.

Directions: From Truro, exit Highway 104 at Glenholme and follow the route along the Bay of Fundy for forty-five minutes. In Parrsboro, follow signs to Ottawa House, drive 3 km (2 mi.) past the Ship's Company Theatre.

Sir Charles Tupper.

Colchester Historical Society Museum

Constructed in 1900 of brick masonry with a red sandstone foundation, this building is a good example of late-Victorian architecture. Originally erected as the Industrial Arts building for the Normal College (Nova Scotia Teacher's College) it houses many permanent and temporary displays about railroading, pioneer life, agriculture, and shipbuilding in the county.

Look for the exhibit about the Londonderry Mines in Londonderry and the many foundries in Colchester County that grew as a result.

There is something for everyone here, including a well equipped research centre, which holds birth, death, and marriage records on microfilm. Also available are early township records, cemetery information, family genealogy and community histories.

Directions: From Highway 104, take the exit to Truro. The Colchester Historical Society Museum is at 29 Young Street, Truro.

Colchester Historical
Society Museum:
(902) 895-6284;
Fax 895-9530
Open year-round
June 1-Sept 30: Tues-
Fri 10 a.m.-5 p.m.;
Sat-Sun 2-5 p.m.
Oct-May 31: Tues-Fri
10 a.m.-noon and 2-5
p.m. Sat 2-5 p.m.

Located in downtown Truro, the museum's exhibits span over a century of the area's industrial and social history.

27

Lawrence House Museum National Historic Site

Lawrence House Museum: (902) 261-2628
Open June 1-Oct 15: Mon-Sat 9:30 a.m.-5:30 p.m.; Sun 1-5:30 p.m.

In Maitland in 1874, William Dawson Lawrence designed the largest full-rigged ship ever built in Canada. It took a workforce of 75 men and weighed in at 2,459 tonnes. A crowd of 4,000 onlookers cheered the christening and official launch of the *W.D. Lawrence.*

Lawrence, the son of Irish immigrants, was elected to the Nova Scotia House of Assembly as a North Hants representative in the 1860s. He had this grand old house built for him and his family. Its style is typical of a captain or shipbuilder's home in the Golden Age of Sail.

The attic is filled with artifacts such as straw hampers, trunks and suitcases, boxes of old pictures, old chairs, rockers, and beds. On the second floor there is a small room from which Lawrence could view his busy shipyard. Downstairs in the kitchen is an old cast-iron stove, a "New Waterloo No. 8" model. There are work areas in which Lawrence designed his vessels. Two large parlours and a dining room, all furnished, round out the tour.

The Lawrence House Museum is located on the shores of Cobequid Bay.

A second floor exhibit features photographs of Maitland-area vessels in the late 1800s and visitors can scan the Minas Basin through viewing scopes.

A special outdoor exhibit provides background on the Lawrence family and their shipbuilding heritage. Miss Abbie Lawrence, William's granddaughter, sold the house and original furnishings to the Province of Nova Scotia. Lawrence House is now part of the Nova Scotia Museum family and has been a National Historic Site since 1965.

Directions: From Truro, exit to Route 236, cross over to Route 215, north to Maitland. From Windsor, take Route 215 to Maitland, approximately 93 km (58 mi.).

William D. Lawrence (top) and his acclaimed *W.D. Lawrence* (bottom).

Little White School House Museum

Little White School
House Museum:
House (902) 893-5170
Open June 1-Aug 31:
Mon-Fri 10 a.m.-6
p.m.; Wed 10 a.m.-8
p.m.

This little schoolhouse is surely the most peripatetic structure in Nova Scotia. Its history as a museum began in 1974 when faculty members at the Nova Scotia Teacher's College—now the Nova Scotia Community College (Truro Campus)—initiated a search for a standing tribute to the teachers of Nova Scotia. They found it in Riverton in a structure built sometime in the mid-1860s. The schoolhouse was moved several times throughout the province before it took its present position on the campus.

The schoolhouse contains books, Dawson school desks, and the *Rules for Teachers.* Stern and rigid, even by Victorian standards, they

were particularly hard on women: "During term of contract, no marrying, no keeping company with men, no smoking, no dressing in bright colours, no hair dyeing, must wear at least two petticoats, and, curiously, "no loitering downtown in any ice cream stores."

The Little White School House Museum, situated on the now Nova Scotia Community College Truro campus.

Directions: The site is on the Nova Scotia Community College (Truro campus), 20 Arthur Street, Truro.

Sunrise Trail

Sunrise Trail

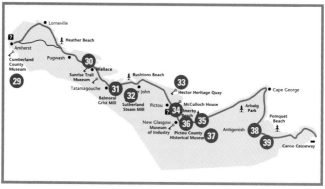

29 Cumberland County Museum

30 Sunrise Trail Museum

31 Balmoral Grist Mill Museum

32 Sutherland Steam Mill Museum

33 Hector Heritage Quay

34 McCulloch House Museum, Hector Archive & Research Centre

35 Loch Broom Log Church

36 The MacPherson's Grist Mill

37 Carmichael-Stewart House Museum

38 Antigonish Heritage Museum

39 St. Augustine's Monastery

Introduction

Following the warm Northumberland Strait coast of Nova Scotia is the Sunrise Trail. From the border town of Amherst to the edge of the Canso Causeway leading to Cape Breton, this area is marked by Scottish immigration in the eighteenth and nineteenth centuries. Note the Scottish names of historic sites along this route: Balmoral, Sutherland, Loch Broom—all names taken from places in the Highlands of Scotland.

Enjoying the Pictou Heritage Festival.

The first major influx of Scots came aboard the *Hector* in 1773, which left Ullapool in northwestern Scotland and creaked into Pictou Harbour several months later. These settlers came to escape poverty and land clearances in Scotland, lured by free passage and the promise of land grants. Many were ill-prepared for what they met: uncleared, forested land. But the Scots were tenacious and not only survived, but prospered as merchants, farmers, writers, educators, and politicians. The town of Antigonish is considered to be the heart of New Scotland, and each year descendants of those Scottish settlers celebrate their heritage with the Antigonish Highland Games, one of the oldest such games in Canada.

Before the Scots, Acadians and Mi'kmaq lived here. You can still see traces of the Acadian dyke system along the route near Tatamagouche. This small village was also a debarkation point for Acadians exiled in 1755.

Cumberland County Museum

Built in 1831, Grove Cottage was the historical home of Senator R.B. Dickey, one of the Fathers of Confederation. Inside this white heritage home, shaded by giant elms and maples, you will find artifacts from the nineteenth century, including historical correspondence, photographs, and memorabilia of some of the great statesmen and reformers of the time: men such as Charles Tupper, who became a prime minister of Canada; Jonathan McCully, who replaced Joseph Howe as editor of the reform newspaper, The *Novascotian*; and Edward Chandler of Amherst, who became a lieutenant-governor of New Brunswick.

Cumberland County Museum
(902) 667-2561
FAX (902)667-0996
Open Oct 1-April 31
Tues-Sat 9 a.m.-5 p.m.
May 1-Sept 30 Mon-Sat 9 a.m.-5 p.m.

A year-round museum, it also presents the natural, industrial, and human history of Cumberland County. The town of Amherst has some fine old houses and municipal buildings made of red sandstone brick with stone foundations worth viewing. Grove Cottage has displays of some of these bricks and stones: Amherst red stone and Wallace grey stone as well as Pugwash brick. The red sandstone deposits in Amherst were developed by James Donalds in the 1880s.

Some varied historical attractions in a tranquil setting at Grove Cottage.

Other attractions include a display of fishing weirs and marshland farm implements, including a wooden shovel, hand sickle, flail, and winnowing pan for wheat harvesting, wooden hay rake, and oxen yoke.

The museum is a designated heritage property and a municipal art gallery. It also contains an archive with extensive records pertaining to the county's cemeteries. The Grove Cottage luncheon is held every June, and an Antique Mechanical Fair takes place on the second Saturday of each August.

A Robb Engine on display at the Cumberland County Museum

Directions: From Highway 101, take Exit 3 to Amherst. Museum is at 150 Church Street.

Sunrise Trail
Museum:
(902) 657-3007
Open daily in
summer months;
weekends only in
late June and early
Sept

From early Mi'kmaq and Acadians who settled in
Tatamagouche to French Huguenots, this museum
has it all. Colonel Frederick Wallet Desbarres,
Lieutenant Governor of Cape Breton Island from
1784 to 1787, was an accomplished surveyor, colo-
nizer, and artist who brought the French
Huguenots over in the mid-1700s.

Scotsman Welwood Waugh arrived here with
his family in 1778. He started the village's first
church, school, and mill. Look for the fine display

Discover the history
of the North Shore
Mi'kmaq, the
Acadians of the area
and of DesBarres
and his first settlers.

of small tools and artifacts used in shipbuilding,
farming, fishing, and forestry. There is plenty of
memorabilia dealing with pioneer life and the early
twentieth-century lifestyles of the inhabitants of
Tatamagouche and the Northumberland shore.

Directions: The Sunrise Trail Museum is on Main
Street in Tatamagouche, along Route 6.

Balmoral Grist Mill Museum

In the 1800s four hundred mills were grinding out critically important supplies of flour, oatmeal, and livestock feed. The Balmoral Grist Mill is a fine working example of the grist mills found in towns and villages across Nova Scotia in the latter half of the nineteenth century.

The mill is situated in a superb natural setting—a deep gorge. The picturesque building, made of rock maple, is the last of five mills on Matheson's Brook grinding oats, barley, wheat, rye, and buckwheat. One of the few operating mills left in the province, it was built around 1874 by Alexander McKay. It is operated by a Leffel turbine on the lower level, but a waterwheel turns in the mill stream for the enjoyment of visitors.

Balmoral Grist Mill:
(902) 657-3016
Open June 1-Oct 15:
Mon-Sat 9:30 a.m.-
5:30 p.m.; Sun 1-5:30 p.m.

Inside, on the main level, are the millstones and related equipment. The window provides a lovely view of the brook and dam. Local granite stone is on display outside; you can see where some of the rock has been removed to make a millstone. The gift shop building once served as a stable.

This is not only a place to observe past technology, but also offers an exciting experience for children. Milling demonstrations take place daily. You may want to finish your visit by crossing the bridge over the brook to lunch at picnic tables, or sit and enjoy the sound of falling water and the view of the gorge. The Christine McDonald Walking Trail leads you along the gorge.

Directions: Follow Route 311 from Tatamagouche, turn left on Route 256. Balmoral Grist Mill is at 660 Matheson Brook Road.

An interpreter takes you through the process of grinding flour, and you will be able to examine the unique Scottish oat-drying kiln. Upstairs are bins from which the grain travels down to the millstones.

Sunrise
Trail

32 **Sutherland Steam Mill Museum**

Sutherland Steam
Mill: (902) 657-3365
Open June 1-Oct 15:
Mon-Sat 9:30 a.m.-
5:30 p.m.; Sun 1-5:30
p.m.

By the late 1800s Nova Scotia had turned from
water to steam in order to run its saw mills. In
1894 Alexander Sutherland chopped down an
enormous virgin hemlock tree and built his steam
mill next to the railway line.

Born in West Branch, Pictou County, Alexander
learned his family trade as a carriage maker. His
brother, Thomas, looked after the house construction part of the business.

Inside the
museum, you can
still see the
machines that
made gingerbread
cut-outs, and that
sanded, and
created mortise-
and-tenon joints.

The main floor was used for general woodwork
and custom jobs. Upstairs, carriages and sleighs were
constructed and painted. Tin-lined wooden tubs,
wagon and carriage wheels, windows and doors were
all made here. In 1940 Alexander retired and his
son, Wilfred, took over the business. During World
War II the mill met a steady demand for lumber,
needed especially in Britain. Wilfred retired and the
mill closed in 1958. The steam is up for the day and
through Saturday, every week. Listen for the sound
of the whistle and see the equipment fashion wood
once more. Sutherland Steam Mill is part of the
Nova Scotia Museum family.

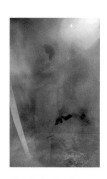

The Sutherland
Steam Mill.

Directions: Follow Route 326 to Denmark, near
Tatamagouche.

Discover
Nova Scotia
Historic Sites

Hector Heritage Quay

Lured by the promise of free land, passage, and provisions for a year, 189 men, women, and children arrived in Pictou from Scotland on the *Hector* in 1773, heralding the start of a wave of Scottish immigrants to Nova Scotia—New Scotland.

The Hector Heritage Quay on the Pictou waterfront is an attractively designed four-storey building containing three floors of exhibits and displays. Accompanying music and the sounds of creaking wooden ships create a haunting tapestry of

Hector Heritage Quay: (902) 485-8028 or 485-4371 Open daily mid May-mid Oct.

the history of those who left Loch Broom, Scotland, including Campbells, MacLeods, Frasers and Sutherlands.

The second-floor display, "Life Below Deck," of the re-creation of the ship is convincing, with figures in costume, barrels, rope coils, and tiers of rough pine-board beds.

Outside is the impressive reconstruction of the original three-masted, ship-rigged *Hector*. The original *Hector*, built in Holland years before the 1773 voyage, was 83 feet long, 24 wide and 10 deep, and the length from bow to stern was 120 feet. A workhorse for the day, the ship came to honour Pictou County as the "Birthplace of New Scotland."

Directions: Exit Highway 104 at Route 106 to Pictou. Heritage Quay is at 33 Caladh Avenue, downtown Pictou.

The ship *Hector* heralded the start of a wave of Scottish immigrants to Nova Scotia giving Pictou its clan names of today. Each clan's tartan is represented in a display inside the Interpretive Centre.

The full scale reproduction of the ship *Hector*, due to launch September 2000, allows visitors to go aboard and experience the passage of 1773.

McCulloch House Museum and Hector Archive & Research Centre

Hector Centre:
(902)485-4563
Open May 16-Oct 29:
Wed-Sat 9:30 a.m.-
5:30 p.m.; Sun 1:30-
5:30 p.m.
McCulloch House is
closed for the 1999
season but re-opens
June 1, 2000. Open
June 1-Oct 15: Mon-
Sat 9:30 a.m.–5:30
p.m.; Sun 1–5:30 p.m.

You can visit the Hector Centre and also see some of the McCulloch artifacts while McCulloch House Museum, part of the Nova Scotia Museum family, undergoes renovations. McCulloch House re-opens in June, 2000.

Imported bricks from Scotland built this early nineteenth-century "Scottish domestic-style" building, home of the Reverend Thomas McCulloch, MD. Considered the father of liberalized education in Nova Scotia, McCulloch was also a renowned author.

A compassionate and tolerant man, his dreams of a non-sectarian college were fully realized when Pictou Academy was incorporated in 1816. McCulloch was named principal of the Academy. In 1838 he became the first president of Dalhousie College in Halifax. Today he is considered a person of national historic significance.

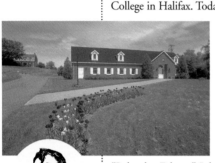

While McCulloch House Museum undergoes renovations, visitors can still see some of McCulloch's possessions, including artifacts and paintings and an original Audubon print, "Labrador Falcon." John James Audubon, the famous American naturalist, made a special trip to Pictou to meet McCulloch. Audubon considered McCulloch's scientific collection the finest of its kind on the continent.

The Hector Centre contains family and community histories, including church, cemetery, census, shipping records, and newspapers. The writings of other prominent Pictonians—intellec-tuals, philosophers, merchants, and missionaries—can be found in the historical collection.

The Hector Centre, pictured above, has an impressive genealogy collection; Reverend Thomas McCulloch (below).

Directions: From Highway 104, exit at Route 106 and follow signs to Pictou. McCulloch House Museum is located at 86 Old Haliburton Road. The Hector Archive and Research Centre is at 100 Old Haliburton Road.

Discover
Nova Scotia
Historic Sites

40

Loch Broom Log Church

A dirt road takes you past a farmhouse and fields to a replica of the first church in Pictou County, built in 1787. The original log structure was 40 feet long by 25 feet wide. The first service was conducted in Gaelic and English by the Rev. James MacGregor, who arrived from Scotland in 1786 to minister to the entire county of Pictou.

This modest place of worship is spartan inside, with long wooden pews, a small altar platform, and a ladder to the loft where young people sat. Outside, look for the large stone etched with a cross and a clan crest in a circle below. The stone is a memorial to all those listed—thirty-seven sets of clans are mentioned, beginning with Chalmers and ending with MacTaylor. It also commemorates the arrival of Alexander Cameron, 1728-1831, born at Loch Broom, Scotland, who witnessed the Battle of Culloden on April 16, 1746. He emigrated on the *Hector* and named his land grant "Loch Broom." His descendants have spread across North America.

Directions: From Highway 104 take Exit 20 onto Route 376, follow signs; the site is near the Loch Broom Bridge at 18 Harbour Crescent.

Loch Broom Log Church:
Open early July-early Sept: Tues-Sat 11 a.m.-6 p.m.; Sun 1-6 p.m. (church service 3 p.m.)

The first service in the Loch Broom Log Church was held in 1787.

The Macpherson's Grist Mill

The Macpherson's Grist Mill is perhaps one of the most charmingly picturesque old structures in the region. Red ivy climbs the weathered, shingled two-storey building, which is topped with a stone chimney. When William Macpherson built his mill in 1861, an overshot wheel provided the power; later an 1880-model water turbine was installed. When the flow of the river was right, William's mill ran night and day grinding out buckwheat, wheat, and oatmeal on its three sets of millstones.

Interpreters explain the working of the mill and the kiln and take visitors through the old farm homestead, with its antique furnishings and artifacts contributed by Pictou County residents.

Directions: Take Exit 26 off Highway 104, onto Route 347 southeast; from New Glasgow, take Route 347, just a few kilometres to the Mill.

Macpherson's Mills:
(902) 752-6266
Open July and Aug.

Sunrise Trail

Carmichael-Stewart House Museum

Carmichael-Stewart
House Museum: (902)
752-5583
Open July-Aug: Mon-
Fri 9 a.m.-4:30 p.m;
Sat 1-4 p.m.

This attractive nineteenth-century Victorian home, shaded by tall trees, was built by James Carmichael—shopkeeper and shipbuilder. In 1809 he opened a general store and so became the founder of New Glasgow. Descendants of the Carmichael family bequeathed the home to the town.

Inside, several rooms are furnished in period

The Pictou County Museum in the heart of the town of New Glasgow.

style. Look for the fine displays of Trenton glass, a flourishing trade from 1881 to 1890, which include pressed glass from the Nova Scotia Glass Company. Upstairs, admire the brightly patterned stained glass windows. Other exhibits emphasize the shipbuilding and mining for which Pictou County became famous.

A Pictou resident dressed in period costume during the Hector Festival.

Directions: Take Exit 26 off Highway 104. Follow Route 347 southeast. The museum is in downtown New Glasgow, at 86 Temperance Street.

Antigonish Heritage Museum

Not many passenger trains exist in Nova Scotia now although they were once essential to carry people, goods, and the mail. But at the turn of the century the railroad was an intrinsic link between towns and villages. Few railway station buildings like this one are left, and with many of the original architectural features of the period remaining, it's an attractive and interesting museum.

Walk around inside and get a feeling of the place, with the waiting room, stationmaster's office, and baggage shed—all memories of daily train travel that still tug at the hearts of Maritimers. In this former railway station there are many fascinating collections: railway memorabilia, pioneer artifacts, photographs, and special exhibits.

In July the annual Antigonish Highland Games are in full swing and you can view displays of Scottish tartans, clans, and history. Also available are genealogical research resources such as cemetery inscriptions, census records, local and family histories. Acadians lived in this historic area but since

Antigonish Heritage
Museum:
(902) 863-6160
Open year-round
July-Aug: Mon-Sat
10 a.m.-5 p.m.;
enquire locally about
off-season hours.

1855 when St. Francis Xavier University was founded, Antigonish has become better known for being a university town.

Directions: Follow Highway 104 to Antigonish; the museum, located at 20 East Main Street, is the former CNR railway station near the downtown area of Antigonish.

Investigate Antigonish's genealogical past at the Antigonish Heritage Museum.

St. Augustine's Monastery

St. Augustine's
Monastery: The
chapel is open
at all times, as is the
outdoor shrine

The two barns
at the back of
the monastery
are no longer
standing.

Originally established as a Trappist monastery in
1825, in what is now the community of Monastery,
this was the first successful monastery in the New
World. On his 1818 missionary journeys to Cape
Breton, Father Vincent de Paul Merle from France
discovered this wooded valley only a half mile from
the sea, and purchased three hundred acres. Father
Vincent, venerated as a saint during his lifetime,
called this place "Petit Clairvaux" after the
Clairvaux cathedral in his native country.

Forty-five Belgian Trappist monks arrived after
Father Vincent to live at the monastery, where they
made and sold butter and cheese. A fire in 1896
destroyed the wooden monastery, mills and work-

Follow the stations of
the cross beside a
woodland path to a
tiny chapel, and a
refreshing waterfall.

shop. The monks were forced to move into an
unfinished shell of a brick monastery they had been
working on; after a few years they moved to Rhode
Island.

After remaining empty for five years, Petit
Clairvaux was taken over by the Abbey of
Thymadeuc in Brittany and occupied by twelve
monks, but it too closed down in 1919.

In 1937, the monastery you see today was
bought by its present occupants, the Augustinian
Fathers, as a refuge for members of their order
expelled from Nazi Germany. Feel free to stroll
around the grounds of the monastery. Visit the
spartan little chapel, which is open to everyone. An
outdoor shrine to Our Lady of Grace is just a short
walk further along the dirt road.

Directions: From Highway 104, take Exit 37 to
Route 4, toward junction with Route 16. Take the
first left on Route 4 (there is a large sign) to the
Monastery, about one mile (1600 metres) along the
dirt road.

Cape Breton Trails

- Ceilidh Trail
40. MacDonald House Museum

- Cabot Trail
41. Alexander Graham Bell National Historic Site
42. Acadian Museum & Dr. Elizabeth LeFort Gallery and Museum

- Bras d'Or Lakes Scenic Drive
43. Nova Scotia Highland Village
44. Orangedale Railway Station Museum

- Fleur-de-lis, Marconi Trails and Trail & Metro Cape Breton

45. Marconi National Historic Site
46. Nicolas Denys Museum & St. Peter's Canal
47. Fortress of Louisbourg National Historic Site
48. St. Patrick's Church Museum; Jost House; Cossit House Museum
49. Cape Breton Miners' Museum

Introduction

Cape Breton Island has a long and turbulent history. Mi'kmaq tribes roamed the area long before John Cabot sailed up the coast in 1497, claiming all he saw for the King of England. Later, in 1534, Jacques Cartier claimed the land for France.

Cape Breton, called Île Royale by the French, was one of the last French territories in North America. The King of France built a mammoth fortress at Louisbourg to defend French interests on the island. Acadian farmers and fishermen, some fleeing English control and mainland Nova Scotia, settled on Cape Breton and traded with the fortress, secure that the fortified town of Louisbourg would offer a safe haven from British soldiers. It was not to be. The fortress fell to the English in 1758 and in 1820 Britain annexed Cape Breton to the colony of Nova Scotia. There are still a number of Acadian villages on Cape Breton, identified by their church spires.

Drummers at
Fortress Louisbourg.

Cape Breton is largely populated by Scottish immigrants who settled here in the one hundred years following the arrival of the *Hector* at Pictou in 1773. Over 50,000 Scottish pioneers arrived in Sydney during the 1800s. Their presence is revealed in the place names: Iona, Barra, Dingwall, Inverness, and Ingonish, and in the Scottish surnames of the residents. There are still a handful of Gaelic speakers on the island, particularly in the Mabou area, and others are discovering the language of their heritage at the Gaelic College in St. Ann's, not far from Baddeck.

The Sydney area of Cape Breton was an important industrial region during the nineteenth and twentieth centuries. In addition to the Scots, Irish labourers arrived to work in the coal mines around Glace Bay. Steel mills were built in Sydney to meet the demand for ships and railroads, and fish processing plants were built all along the coast.

Cape Breton was also witness to some exciting scientific discoveries in the early 1900s. On Bras d'Or Lake (Canada's largest inland sea), Alexander Graham Bell built his summer home, developed the hydrofoil boat, and designed the Silver Dart, two highly successful projects of Bell's Aerial Experiment Association. On the outskirts of Glace Bay, Guglielmo Marconi transmitted the world's first wireless message.

St. Patrick's Church in Sydney.

Today, with the closure of the fishery, steel mills, and coal mines, the economy of Cape Breton is in decline. But it is still a tourist mecca with beautiful scenery, attractive villages, the famed Bras d'Or Lakes, and historic sites that commemorate the island's colourful past.

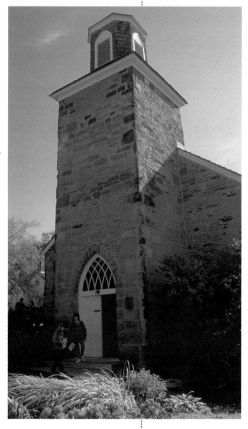

MacDonald House:
(902) 258-3317
Open June 15-Sept 15:
Daily 9 a.m.-9 p.m.

Highland cattle
graze on the
museum's property.

Alexander MacDonald chose this superb setting for his homestead—a hillside overlooking Lake Ainslie, the largest natural freshwater lake in Nova Scotia. A native weaver from the Isle of Mull, Scotland, Alexander married Mary MacLean. They had four girls and two boys.

Charles, the second son, established the area's first mercantile business in 1848, and built this house in the mid-1850s. The Gothic-revival dwelling is white with green trim, with a steeply pitched roof and gingerbread trim above the front entrance. The community's first post office opened here—with Charles as the first postmaster—and remained in service until 1956.

Inside the old farmhouse there is an interesting display of furniture and artifacts, including two pre-1830 pioneer chairs and an antique loom. Look for the

The little 1920s one-room schoolhouse has been relocated to this site and is furnished with two-seater desks, old textbooks, and other memorabilia.

implement building, which contains an impressive array of farm machinery, horse-drawn buggies, sleighs, and wagons. The 1928 barn is used for displays and barn dances during the summer months.

Directions: Take Highway 105 to Route 395. The Museum is located on Route 395 in East Lake Ainslie, overlooking Lake Ainslie.

Alexander Graham Bell
National Historic Site

After the construction of Beinn Bhreagh Hall, their 34-room, brick-red "summer castle" overlooking Baddeck Bay, Alexander Graham Bell and his wife, Mabel, used it all their lives as a second permanent home. It was here that Bell, inventor of the telephone, and his assistant Casey Baldwin carried out important experiments in the field of aviation.

Although the house itself is not open to the public, Bell's eclectic life and work are revealed in the nearby museum, which contains the world's largest collection of artifacts and archives commemorating this extraordinary man.

Begin your tour with a bank of videos about the life of "Alec," as Mabel called him. Look for a wall of photographs and interpretations devoted to Bell's work with the deaf. Be sure to view the film that includes the meeting between Alec and Mabel Hubbard, who was deaf and sixteen years old when she became Alexander's pupil.

Photographs and films show how Bell experimented with the possibilities of aerial flight, beginning with kites. Bell launched the first gasoline-powered aircraft in the British Empire, here at Baddeck. Discover his brilliant development of the hydrofoil boat which, in1908, driven by air propellers, rose one foot above the water.

Alexander Graham Bell and his wife Mabel had an abiding love for their second home and cherished such heartfelt memories of Baddeck that they chose to be buried at Beinn Bhreagh.

Directions: Take Exit 9 off Highway 105. The site is located at the east end of the village of Baddeck on Chebucto Street (Route 205).

Alexander Graham
Bell National
Historic Site
(902) 295-2069
Open year-round
June: 9 a.m.-6 p.m.
July 1-Aug 1:
8:30 a.m.-7:30 p.m.
Sept 1-Oct 15:
8:30 a.m.-6:00 p.m.
Oct 16-May 31:
9:00 a.m.-5:00 p.m.

Bell spent 37 summers in Cape Breton, the most beautiful place he said he had ever visited.

Alexander Graham Bell pioneered numerous innovations, from the hydrofoil boat to the telephone.

Acadian Museum & Dr. Elizabeth LeFort Gallery and Museum: Les Trois Pignons

Acadian Museum:
(902) 224-2170
Open June 15-Sept
30: 8 a.m.-9 p.m.
May 15-June 15 &
Oct 1-25: 9 a.m.-
6 p.m.
LeFort Museum:
(902) 224-2642 or 224-
2612
Open May-Oct:
Mon-Fri 9 a.m.-5 p.m.
July-Aug: Daily 9
a.m.-6 p.m.

Chéticamp is a
must for fans of rug
hooking. The
tradition remains
very much alive
today.

Not far from one entrance to the Cape Breton Highlands National Park, the bilingual settlement of Chéticamp stretches along the Cabot Trail. Fish plants line the main street, and at one time inhabitants could catch fish almost from their doorsteps.

In 1790 exiled Acadians returned from the French islands of St. Pierre and Miquelon and established Chéticamp. The museum displays antiques and artifacts pertaining to their culture. Downstairs, a young woman in Acadian costume demonstrates weaving. There is a reconstructed ancient chapel with vestments, candleholders, and an organ. Period rocking chairs, washtubs, spinning wheels, and a cast-iron stove all catch the eye.

Be sure to visit Les Trois Pignons, a community centre with cultural and genealogical information. Here, the Elizabeth LeFort Gallery displays twenty of the three hundred magnificent hooked tapestries by Chéticamp native, Dr. LeFort, who is considered Canada's top wool artist. Her works are spread far and wide; some are in the Vatican in Rome, the White House in Washington, DC, Buckingham Palace in London, and the Canadian Museum of Civilization in Ottawa.

The reconstructed chapel.

Directions: From Highway 105, exit at Route 19 to 744 Main Street, Chéticamp, for the Acadian Museum. The LeFort Gallery and Museum is across the street from Acadian Museum.

Acadian Museum: 🚻 P $
LeFort: 🚻 P $

Nova Scotia Highland Village

The Highland Village at Iona chronicles the lives of Highland Scots on Cape Breton. Spread out over forty-three hilly acres, a series of ten buildings overlooks the Bras d'Or Lakes. The outdoor pioneer museum presents a 180-year chronology of the history of Scottish settlers on Cape Breton.

Highland Village:
(902) 725-2272;
Fax 725-2227
Village: Open June 1-
Oct 5: Mon-Sat 9 a.m.-
5 p.m.; Sun 10 a.m.-6
p.m.
Interpretive Centre:
Open year-round:
Mon-Fri 9 a.m.-5 p.m.

The historic stroll begins with an uphill path leading to the Black House—Taigh Dubh in Gaelic—lived in by native Gaels in Scotland. Built mostly of stone, this re-creation of a croft house is the only one in North America. It has walls six feet thick, with a thatched or sod roof, fireplace, and a smoke-hole in the roof. Peat burned in the fireplace and the Black House gets its name from the soot that covered the inner walls. Inside, look for a byre, which held small animals (a pony, cow, sheep, or goat). The main living area has a press, or cupboard, used as storage or as a sleeping area. Next to the house is a garden for potatoes and kale.

Along the rambling gravel paths you'll find the following: an 1810 log house; the MacDonald frame house of 1829; a nineteenth-century farm with a sterling collection of carriages— including a hearse and a dog treadmill; the middle-class MacQuarrie/Fox home (c.1865); the Whycocomagh/Portage School House (c.1920)— with desks, books, maps, and slates; a forge, store, and carding mill; and the 1900 MacIvor/Nash House.

Some of the houses you will see at the Highland Village. The Village has a spectacular view (bottom).

Directions: Follow Route 223 for 19 km (12 mi.) east of Highway 105; take Exit 6 to Iona.

Orangedale Railway Station Museum

Orangedale Railway
Station Museum:
(902) 756-3384
Open mid-June-mid-
Oct: Mon-Sat 10 a.m.-
6 p.m.; Sun 1-6 p.m.

This fine nineteenth-century station was destined for the rubble heap after train service was discontinued in 1990, but fortunately it was saved by caring citizens. Constructed of solid wood timber in 1886, the structure is painted red with cream trim, restoring the station to its former splendour. It is the last remaining station of seventeen built for the Intercolonial Railway of Canada. The station stands on its original site and several railway cars are parked nearby on the now rusting tracks.

Inside the station, rail buffs will find an operating model railroad. You can sense another age as

you stroll around the large office, waiting rooms, and the station master's apartment with its original furniture. The museum displays artifacts, memorabilia, and railroad data on the cultural and historical aspects of the rail line through Cape Breton Island. Stop upstairs to have a cup of tea in the dining room.

Orangedale was
once a busy
transportation
centre, channeling
the rail traffic
between Baddeck,
Sydney, Louisbourg
and mainland Nova
Scotia.

Directions: From Highway 105 take Exit 4 to the community of Orangedale. The museum is also accessible by water; a government wharf on the Bras d'Or Lakes is close by.

From this plateau of jutting barren land at Table Head in Glace Bay you are as close as anywhere to the edge of the world. It was from this point on December 15, 1902, that the Italian inventor, Guglielmo Marconi transmitted the first trans-Atlantic wireless message to Poldhu, England. It was a triumph of newly developed wireless telegraphy—the beginning of the dawn of modern global communications.

Marconi National Historic Site: (902) 295-2069 (year-round); 842-2530 (summer only). Open June 1-Sept 15: Daily 10 a.m.-6 p.m.

Nothing remains of the station except the concrete foundations of the station itself and the square concrete tower foundations, marked at strategic points by three interpretive panels, but you can imagine the enormous 210-foot (64-metre) towers overlooking the ocean, with hundreds of copper antenna cables attached to them.

Inside the exhibit centre you can learn all about the "Wizard of Wireless." Centre stage is a large, carefully detailed scale model of the original wireless station, complete with aerial array, buildings, towers, and topography of the Table Head site.

Here you can learn about Marconi the inventor and Marconi the man.

There is a fascinating screen presentation made of black and white stills, pieces of old film, interviews, and sounds. Printed material is available in the second exhibit area, along with helpful interpretive staff at the information counter. Amateur radio club aficionados will be happy to discover "Station VAS" behind the counter. This radio station is operated by the Sydney Amateur Radio Club members, who send and receive messages from all over the world.

Marconi went on to work more with short-wave systems and in 1927 the "Beam System" began to link the entire British Empire. He was referred to as "Marconi the Merlin," and part of his phenomenal success took place here at Table Head.

Guglielmo Marconi

Directions: The site is located in Glace Bay at Table Head, on Timmerman Street. Take Route 4 from Sydney to Glace Bay (23 km or 15 mi.); driving time is thirty minutes. Or take scenic Route 255, the Marconi Trail, from Louisbourg (51 km or 32 mi.); driving time is one hour.

Nicolas Denys Museum & St. Peter's Canal

Long before the canal was built, the Mi'kmaq people had to portage their canoes over this narrow isthmus between the Bras d'Or Lakes and St. Peter's Bay. Peripatetic Portuguese fishermen called it San Pedro. Nicolas Denys, a seventeenth-century merchant from LaRochelle, France, took possession of the settlement in 1650 and called it Saint Pierre. A Renaissance man, Denys was part trader, part explorer, and part entrepreneur. He was also involved in the timber export business and a partner in an inshore fishery at Port du Rossignol (Liverpool). Seeing the value of an easier route for

Denys Museum:
Open June 1-Sept 30:
Daily 9 a.m.-5 p.m.
St. Peter's Canal:
(902)733-2280
Open year-round

Overlooking St. Peter's Canal, the Nicolas Denys Museum houses a collection of local historical items, including a display on the life of Nicolas Denys.

the shipment of men and goods, he constructed the first passage for boats across the isthmus in 1699. The old portage trail became a "haulover" road, and oxen, horses, or humans would haul Denys' ships from one shore to another. After a fire destroyed both Saint Pierre and Denys' buildings, a new French settlement, Port Toulouse, became a major supply centre for Louisbourg, about 75 miles (120 km) north along the coastline. The British destroyed the French settlement in 1758, built a new one, and renamed it St. Peter's.

Work on the present canal began in 1854 and took fifteen years of cutting and blasting. Once locks were installed in 1869, the canal was in business. Today you can stroll about, bring a lunch, and view the canal with its traffic of canoes, power cruisers, and schooners. Rarely does a commercial vessel pass through the locks.

Interpretive panels explain how the canal works: St. Peter's Canal connects two bodies of water, each with levels that change at different times and to different degrees. For this reason it is one of the few canals in North America to employ a tidal lock to compensate for the constantly changing water levels between the Bras d'Or Lakes and the Atlantic Ocean. Adjacent to the canal is Battery Provincial

Deny's: Museum:
St. Peter's Canal: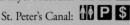

Park, with ocean frontage on the locks. From here you can climb Mount Granville, the highest point in the region, to see the sparse ruins of Fort Dorchester, built by the British in 1793. Over the years the locks have played a vital role in the economy and communications of Cape Breton Island.

The Denys Museum, housed in a French-style building inspired by the trading post established here by Nicolas, is just a brief walk along the west bank of the canal. Artifacts include an eclectic array of memorabilia, a photographic exhibit of the canal's construction, and a display on the life of Nicolas Denys.

Directions: Follow Highway 104 from Port Hawkesbury to St. Peter's. The museum is at 46 Denys Street, overlooking St. Peter's Canal.

Three views of St. Peter's Canal.

Fortress of Louisbourg
National Historic Site

Fortress of
Louisbourg: (902) 733-
2280
Open June & Sept:
9:30 a.m.-5 p.m.
July-Aug 3l: 9 a.m.-
7 p.m.

The Fortress of Louisbourg may well have been
France's greatest military folly in the New World.
Built at great expense as a fortified town in the
early 1700s to protect French interests on Cape
Breton in the face of British soldiers approaching
by sea, it was considered impregnable. But it wasn't.
Louisbourg was captured twice—in 1745 by New
Englanders and in 1758 by the British.

This magnificent historic site—the largest
reconstructed colonial town in North America—
takes a full day for a complete tour, but after four
hours you will have some vivid images to take
home.

As you stroll the
grounds at
Louisbourg, you will
meet a host of
characters dressed
in period costume.

The fortress lies opposite the modern town of
Louisburg at the south entrance to the harbour.
You leave your car at the reception centre and take
a short bus ride to the Maison DesRoches, once the
dwelling place of fisherman George DesRoches. A
brief walk takes you to Dauphin Gate where you
will be "challenged" by seedy-looking soldiers in
blue and white uniforms to declare your nationa-
lity. Go through the portals and you are back in
1740s Louisbourg, a thriving, bustling seaport and
capital of the French Colony of Île Royale (Cape
Breton). There are sixty-five listed buildings (some
still under construction) and locations, including
the Rodrigue House (Children's Interpretive
Centre) and the Duhaget House, with its fifteen-
minute video about a Louisbourg soldier's life and

an exhibition of how the Fortress was built and operated.

Feel free to wander in any direction. Go round the point to where batteries of cannons face out to sea. Roam through the Artillery Storehouse and stop at the King's Bakery to buy a round loaf of oven-fresh bread from a young baker. Animators go about their activities without fanfare. Children and adults toss balls on a rooftop and catch them with their hats. A group of wandering musicians and dancers cavort on the original French cobblestones. A soldier demonstrates loading and firing his rifle. At Pierre Lorant's L'Hotel de la Marine a working-class lunch can be eaten with a pewter spoon—bring your own cutlery!

A brightly attired drummer, easily recognized amidst other members of the military.

Go through the Place d'armes portal and into the King's Bastion and Barracks. This is the largest building on the site and in its day was one of the largest buildings in North America. Inside there is a simple chapel and the apartments of Governor Jean Baptiste Louis Le Prevost, Seigneur du Quesnel, whose remains are buried under the chapel. In the museum section archaeology exhibits are carefully preserved under glass. At the rear of the building is the King's Bastion, a fort within a fort.

Go out into the town again and you can visit the historic gardens and a stable with horses; live animals inside the fortress include goats, pigs, hens, roosters, and swallows swooping in and out of open buildings. Other sites include the parade square, the De La Valliere Storehouses, the Engineer's House (with open-hearth cooking), the Carrerot House (depicting eighteenth-century reconstruction techniques), and the Beausejour House, with animated games and pastimes.

Meanwhile, there is the sound of drummers and shouted orders. Sentries file up and down and clammy fog drifts in from the sea to cling to the massive stone gate and walls, to add an authentic atmosphere to your visit.

The church at Louisbourg.

Directions: The site is located south of Sydney on Route 22, just beyond the modern village of Louisbourg. Take Exit 8 off Route 4. Driving time is thirty minutes. An alternate route is the scenic and coastal Marconi Trail, Route 255, from Glace Bay; driving time is one hour.

48

St. Patrick's Church Museum; Jost House; Cossit House Museum.

St. Patrick's Museum:
(902) 562-8237
Open mid-June-Sept
30: Daily 9:30 a.m.-
5:30 p.m.

Jost House:
(902) 539-0366
Open year-round
July-Aug: Mon-Sat
10 a.m.-4 p.m.
Sept-June: Tues-Fri
10 a.m.-4 p.m.;
Sun 1-4 p.m.

Cossit House:
(902) 539-7973
Open June 1-Oct 15:
Mon-Sat 9:30 a.m.-
5:30 p.m.;
Sun 1-5:30 p.m.

Sydney is one of the oldest settlements in North America. It is home to the Mi'kmaq people and was a refuge for Basque fishermen in the sixteenth century, who called this area Spanish Bay. Loyalists chose this site for a colonial capital around 1785. In the nineteenth century it became a port of entry for 50,000 Scots who settled in Cape Breton. With its huge steelworks, Sydney became an important twentieth century North American industrial centre.

Today you can discover some of the remaining colonial buildings within easy walking distance from downtown Sydney. To arrive at the historical North End, walk along Esplanade in the direction of the Government Wharf; the first site, St. Patrick's Church Museum, is between York and Amelia Streets. Erected in 1812, this fine old building is the oldest Roman Catholic Church on Cape Breton Island. Made of stones and wood, all hand-hewn by Sydney's early residents, it stands as a fine example of the pioneer Gothic style of architecture, and was one of the earliest houses of worship in the city. The church was restored by the Old Sydney Society and now serves as a museum housing local historic memorabilia.

Head up Amelia Street to the Jost House (1787), one of the oldest remaining wooden buildings in Sydney. This is a charming dwelling with the basement restored to an original eighteenth-century kitchen, including a cooking fireplace, a beehive bake-oven, and a plastered ceiling supported by beams. Samuel Sparrow, the merchant and ship owner who owned the property from 1786 to 1787, would have been impressed with the restoration. In 1836 Halifax merchant Thomas Jost bought the property, and his descendants lived here until 1971.

On the ground floor look for furnishings and artifacts in the parlour, the bedroom, dining room, and store. Upstairs is an apothecary shop with a

St. Patrick's is the oldest Roman Catholic church in Cape Breton.

display of utensils used to prepare prescriptions. There is also a marine display and special collections. Don't miss the Ballem Tapestries. Each unique and beautiful artwork, created with wool and silks, took three years to complete by two of the six daughters in the Ballem family. Their father, John Ballem, was a successful businessman, and his daughters travelled on his ships, bringing back with them materials to be used in their tapestries. Their work incorporates a very old stitching technique called Point de Marque, known as "Opus Purvinarium" to the ancient Phygians and Egyptians. Upon completion, these tapestries were exhibited in Europe, Australia, and the United States.

Cossit House Museum, also built in 1787, is just around the corner at 75 Charlotte Street. Reverend Ranna Cossit arrived in Sydney from New Hampshire in 1786. He brought with him his wife, Thankful Brooks. Eventually, their family included thirteen children. Cossit was the first Anglican minister assigned to permanent duty in Cape Breton. He built his one-and-a-half-storey, wood-

en framed, gable-roofed home. Costumed guides greet you as you enter the front hall. All rooms are furnished in eighteenth-century style, and some of the furniture on exhibit is based on the 1815 inventory of Cossit's estate. Cossit House Museum is operated by the Old Sydney Society for the Nova Scotia Museum.

Directions: Take Exit 20 off Highway 105, and follow Highway 125 to Sydney. St. Patrick's Museum is at 87 Esplanade; Jost House is at 54 Charlotte Street; and Cossit House is at 75 Charlotte Street.

At Jost House you can see the evolution of a family home from 1785 to 1900.

Cape Breton Miners'
Museum:
(902) 849-4522
or 849-8022
Open year-round
June-Sept: Daily
10 a.m.-6 p.m.; Tues
10 a.m.-7 p.m.
Sept-May: Mon-Fri
9 a.m.-4 p.m.

The main building of this Museum Complex in Glace Bay focuses on the geological development of the Sydney coalfields and the many techniques used to mine the seams since 1720. Exhibits include a mock-up of the carboniferous forests that became coal, mine rescue gear, and tools.

You may never be the same again after a guided tour of the Ocean Deeps Colliery, an underground mine located beneath the main building. Wearing a hardhat, and coat, you follow a retired miner for a twenty-minute excursion into a 1932 "room and pillar" mine, where you experience what miners had to go through to extract coal deep down in the black bowels of the earth.

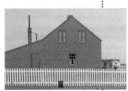

Back on the surface, you are seated in a modern man-rake and—with a video and special effects—travel on a fifteen-minute simulated journey into a present-day coal mine, "Phalen Colliery." Operated by the Cape Breton Development Corporation, although scheduled for closure, it is one of the most modern coal operations in the world. Take time to attend an evening concert by North America's most famous coal mining chorus, the Men of the Deeps.

A visit to the Miners' Museum will provide a vivid look at the arduous life of mining.

Outside, once your tour is over, visit the company store and company house on display. Interpreters make it clear to visitors how much miners and their families were dependent on the company for their homes, their food, and their livelihoods.

Directions: From Sydney, take Route 4 to Glace Bay. The museum is located at Quarry Point off South Street, at 42 Birkley Street, Glace Bay.

Marine Drive

Marine Drive

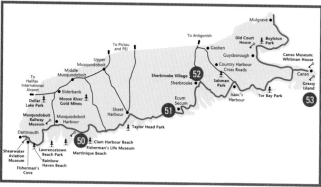

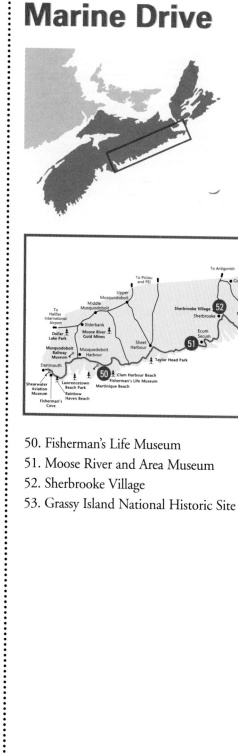

50. Fisherman's Life Museum
51. Moose River and Area Museum
52. Sherbrooke Village
53. Grassy Island National Historic Site

Introduction

Winding its way along Nova Scotia's Eastern Shore, the Marine Drive meanders between forests and the coast, interspersed with small villages perched on rocky outcrops. There was some forestry and mining (including the closed gold mines at Moose River), but most of the pioneers who settled this region turned to fishing for a living. Hence, it is appropriate that a tour of the Marine Drive begin with a visit to the Fisherman's Life Museum at Oyster Pond, which commemorates the harsh life of a typical fisherman and his family.

An idyllic scene at Canso.

Fisherman's Life Museum

To enter this small but cosy fisherman's house is to be gently nudged back in time. The aroma of baking permeates the dwelling. An interpreter, costumed in long dress, pushes a hot flat-iron to smooth fresh laundry. You feel as though you have entered a neighbour's home, and soon yarns and stories will begin to unfold.

Fisherman's Life Museum:
(902) 889-2053
Open June 1-Oct 15:
Mon-Sat 9:30 a.m.-
5:30 p.m.;
Sun 1-5:30 p.m.

James Myers (1834-1915) acquired eight acres of land here around 1850 and worked hard as a fisherman. His youngest son, Ervin, inherited the property in 1907. A fisherman like his father, but with a growing family to support—thirteen daughters in all—Ervin also worked in the Musquodoboit Valley as a lumber camp cook.

Seaweed mulch, manure, and lobster carcasses were used as fertilizer in the vegetable garden. It is here to the east of the house where the family raised root crops for pickling, canning, and storing for winter. Ervin's wife Ethelda took care of the girls and maintained the house while he spent a week at a time fishing and trapping lobsters—often rowing his dory ten miles a day—and landing his catch on Roger-Barren Islands. It was a spartan life, but the large family was well fed. Besides the kitchen, dining room and parlour, there are two bedrooms on the main floor. Upstairs are three bedrooms, one with three large beds.

Fisherman James Myers raised thirteen children in this house.

After warming up by the cookstove, you might want to discover how to hook rugs or knit a raised-leaf bedspread pattern. Outside, stroll down to the edge of Navy Pool to a fish house and a wharf. Oyster Pond, from which the community takes its name, is at the head of the peninsula. On your way past the barn you may hear the bleating of lambs. The Fisherman's Life Museum is a fine illustration of the way of life of the inshore fisherman at the turn of the century on the Eastern Shore. It is part of the Nova Scotia Museum family.

Directions: The museum is located at 58 Navy Pool Loop in Jeddore. Follow Route 7 and exit at Oyster Pond, halfway between Musquodoboit Harbour and Ship Harbour.

Moose River and
Area Museum:
(902) 384-3157
Open June-Labour
Day: Mon-Sat 10
a.m.-5 p.m.;
Sun 11 a.m.-6 p.m.

While hunting moose in 1858 on the Tangier River, Lieutenant L'Estrange discovered gold. And in 1861 an influx of prospectors arrived. The rush and boom of the gold industry took off fifteen years later in 1890. By 1904 there were two gold mines, a lumber business, two hotels, and a population of one hundred. But the boom was short-lived. By 1910 gold mining in Nova Scotia had gone into decline.

In 1936 two Toronto men, heading a gold mine syndicate, and the timekeeper entered the unstable mineshaft to carry out explorations. The mine caved in and the men were trapped. Men from other mines in Nova Scotia and Ontario rallied to undertake a rescue under the most dangerous conditions. It took ten intense and dramatic days to bring the trapped men out of the mine. Two survived; one died after rescue. The gripping story was broadcast live on the air—day by day, hour by hour—by J. Frank Willis over the Canadian radio network. This event made J. Frank Willis famous; his reports were carried by more than seven hundred radio stations in Canada, the United States, and England.

The museum tells the story of the famous mine disaster of 1936.

The pleasant little provincial park established in 1986 is surrounded by trees, bushes, plants, and flowers. Look for the cairn marking the location where the three men were entombed during the collapse of the mine. To one side you can see a large steel structure; it is a century-old five stamp mill used during the late nineteenth century to extract gold from ore.

Directions: Follow Route 1 to Sheet Harbour, then take Route 224 and follow it through Upper Musquodoboit and Centre Musquodoboit to Elmsvale; turn left at the Moose River Road. Continue past Newcomb Corners to Moose River Gold Mines and the provincial park.

Sherbrooke Village

In the mid-1600s, a handful of French pioneers settled here; English immigrants arrived in 1815 and called the village Sherbrooke. Timber, farming and fishing were the main industries until the 1860s, when the discovery of gold energized the town. The boom lasted about twenty years.

Today the restored village is as it was in the nineteenth century, with twenty-five historic buildings open to visitors. People in period costume invite you into the 1850s post office, a printer's shop, and an old-time pharmacy with its pestle and mortar and collections of coloured glass vessels. The ever-popular Cumminger Bros. 1870s general store is a must-see, with its penny candy and wooden boxes and barrels. Two cottages deserve a visit: the Renova Cottage (c. 1850) and Greenwood Cottage (c. 1871), a "showplace of the village." Take time to visit the Coach Barn that once held horses, mail coaches, and express wagons; the 1862 jail; a boat-building shop; the telephone exchange; an 1858 court-house; a church and the company store

Down the road visit the reconstructed nineteenth-century up-and-down sawmill and a lumber camp. Sherbrooke Village is part of the Nova Scotia Museum family.

Directions: Follow Route 7 to Sherbrooke.

Sherbrooke Village
(902) 522-2400 or
1-888-743-7845
(toll free)
Open June 1-Oct 15:
Daily 9:30 a.m.-5:30 p.m. Admission charged.

Originally settled by the French, the village was later named by the English to honour Lieutenant-Governor Sir John Sherbrooke.

Grassy Island National Historic Site

Grassy Island
National Historic
Site: (902) 295-2069
or 366-3136
(summer only)
Open June 1-Sept 15:
Daily 10 a.m.-6 p.m.

This site tells the gripping story of a once thriving community on Grassy Island, just off the Canso coast. In the 1600s, the French came to the Canso islands for the abundance of cod, but were driven out of Canso by the British in 1720. New Englanders were the next to arrive and settle on Grassy Island, establishing a prosperous fishing business by exporting to European markets. In 1744 the French attacked the settlement, looting and burning it. Although the New Englanders retaliated a year later, they never returned to Grassy Island.

Today the windswept little island still carries physical evidence of the early settlers. The Grassy

Island Visitor Centre offers a short video on the island's history (captioned for the hearing impaired). There is also a scale model of the island and a display of eighteenth-century artifacts from the settlement, including cut crystal, stoneware mugs, and fragments of bottles, jars, and clay tobacco pipes.

Grassy Island,
where the rich
fishing waters
created prosperity
for the area.

A short boat tour trip takes you to the island where you will need the small tour pamphlet to introduce you to the the archaeological remains. Along the circular trail there are many properties, including a fort and a church. Look closely and you will see scattered rubble mounds, cellar pits, and

barely visible terraces. Here a stony mound with two cellar pits marks the site of the house of the fish merchant John Trevett. Beside it lies the property of the merchant Edward How, who had the biggest wharf on the island, and, later, John Elliot's place, where cod was laid to dry on the flakes. The remains of widow Anne Crosby's property is next. Nearby are plots owned by two garrison officers, John Jephson and Patrick Heron.

Directions: From Sherbrooke take Route 211, which becomes Route 316. Follow route 316 and turn right on Route 16. A 16 km (10 mi.) drive brings you to the Canso waterfront on Union Street. From Port Hawkesbury take Route 344, which connects with Route 16 off Highway 104 from Antigonish to reach Canso.

🚻 ♿ 🅿 partial ⛱ 💲 ❓ 🔶

Halifax Metro Area

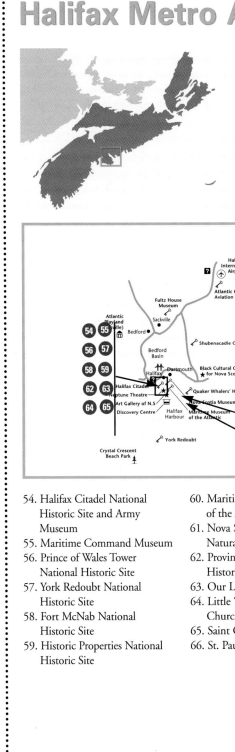

54. Halifax Citadel National Historic Site and Army Museum
55. Maritime Command Museum
56. Prince of Wales Tower National Historic Site
57. York Redoubt National Historic Site
58. Fort McNab National Historic Site
59. Historic Properties National Historic Site

60. Maritime Museum of the Atlantic
61. Nova Scotia Museum of Natural History
62. Province House National Historic Site
63. Our Lady of Sorrows Chapel
64. Little "Dutch" (Deutsch) Church
65. Saint George's Round Church
66. St. Paul's Anglican Church

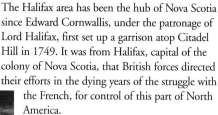

The Halifax area has been the hub of Nova Scotia since Edward Cornwallis, under the patronage of Lord Halifax, first set up a garrison atop Citadel Hill in 1749. It was from Halifax, capital of the colony of Nova Scotia, that British forces directed their efforts in the dying years of the struggle with the French, for control of this part of North America.

The Halifax Town Clock.

Cornwallis and his troops were attracted by the natural, easily defended, ice-free harbour, and behind it the Bedford basin with its deep anchorage for naval fleets. The harbour, above all else, has guided the development of the three main districts of the regional municipality: Halifax, Dartmouth, and Bedford.

It was here that troops and supplies could be brought inshore for British defences during the late1700s. By the 1800s a defence system ringed the mouth of the harbour—from McNab's Island on the Dartmouth side to York Redoubt, not far from Chebucto Head. Interestingly, no shot was ever fired at the enemy and not even a single German U-boat penetrated the submarine net slung across the harbour entrance during World War II.

Halifax remained a garrison town during the late 1800s with thousands of immigrants from Europe and the United States first stepping foot in Canada at the Halifax piers, many of whom remained, so that by the middle of the twentieth century Halifax had become a cosmopolitan metropolis.

Although shipping and trade have remained important to the region, since World War II Halifax has also become a centre for banking and commerce. After the war, a bridge was built across the harbour connecting Halifax and its twin city of Dartmouth. New container facilities were built so that goods from around the world could be offloaded in Halifax and then sent all over Canada.

Boasting six universities, education has been an important factor of life in Halifax. The city is also the birthplace of responsible government, whereby men such as Joseph Howe convinced the British government that the province's citizens should be able to elect their own representatives to enact and enforce local laws.

Over the past 250 years there have been tremendous changes in Halifax. The region's many historic buildings, fortifications, churches, and museums invite visitors to explore its turbulent past.

Halifax Citadel National Historic Site & Army Museum

The present citadel with its star-shaped fortress was designed by Colonel Gustavus Nicolls in 1830-32. Other citadel structures dated back to 1749, when a wooden stockaded fort defended the then new town of Halifax. The third citadel was an imposing octagonal blockhouse, but when Prince Edward, later the Duke of Kent arrived in 1794, he built the rectangular earthen fort with four bastions, surrounded by a ten-foot-deep trench. Sharp palisades were added to discourage attackers.

Prince Edward was renowned for the buildings he commissioned in and around Halifax, including the Prince of Wales Tower in Point Pleasant Park, St. George's round church, eighteenth-century improvements to York Redoubt, and the Music Rotunda on the Bedford Highway.

The large building you see upon entry to the fortress is the Cavalier Building, also designed by Nicolls. Originally a two-storey building, its flat roof held seven 24-pounder guns. Later the gun platform was removed and an extra barrack space was built.

Look for the garrison cell with its narrow cots, firewood bin, and small stove for warmth. Other attractions include the restored powder magazine, wood-lined and able to hold around 2,000 oak barrels, with 90 pounds of black powder in each. There are guides and animators to interpret the musket gallery, guardroom, barracks and schoolroom. "The Tides of History" audio-visual program presents a vivid and stirring account of the citadel and Halifax.

Also visit the Army Museum, with its changing display of military effects including weapons, medals, and uniforms.

Experience the changing of the guard and the Royal Artillery traditional firing of the noon-day gun, a 32-pounder cannon, and a costumed historical re-enactment of life at the citadel.

Directions: Situated on Citadel Hill above the Clock Tower in downtown Halifax. The site can be entered by climbing steps leading to the Clock Tower or from Sackville Street.

Halifax Citadel,
Citadel Hill, Halifax
(902) 426-5080
Army Museum
(902)422-5979
Citadel:
Open May 7-June 30:
9 a.m.-5 p.m.
July 1-Aug 31: 9 a.m.-
6 p.m.
Sept 1-Oct 31: 9 a.m.-
5 p.m.
Museum:
Open as above

Halifax's military history is illuminated by a tour of the citadel's musket gallery, barracks and schoolroom.

Army Museum: 👥 ♿ 🅿 $?
Halifax Citadel: ♿ 🅿 📷 $? 🎧

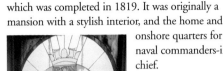

Admiralty House, CFB
Halifax, Stadacona
location, Halifax
(902) 427-0550,
Ext 8250; Fax 427-
2218
Open year-round:
Mon-Fri 9:30 a.m.-
3:30 p.m.

The collection of
artifacts at this
museum reflect the
daily "personal" side
of naval life, more
than weaponry.

Admiralty House is a Georgian-style stone structure which was completed in 1819. It was originally a mansion with a stylish interior, and the home and

onshore quarters for naval commanders-in-chief.

You will find the museum full of artifacts relating to the history of Canada's naval forces during war and peace. On the basement level, look for ship models of World War I and II vintage. There are displays of uniforms, Royal Navy officers' swords, medals, an array of cocked hats, and a Chart Depot office. As you mount the stairs, note the photographic display on the wall of navy crews and ships from both wars.

On the second floor there are more naval swords, weapons of the ship's company, small arms, cutlasses, dirks, boarding pikes, and a blunderbuss (a small gun with a wide muzzle used for close fire). Other features include rifles, musket balls, paintings of ships, and ship's diaries and journals. Visit the "Canada at War" room. The top floor features a submarine escape tower, as well as submarine artifacts.

In the last century the grounds were landscaped and garden parties were held at Admiralty House, with hundreds of guests invited to the fancy balls. As you roam through the museum rooms notice the plaster moulding in the ceiling friezes, fireplace mantels of carved wood and marble, and the mahogany doors, all signs of the original Georgian decor. Admir-alty House is an appropriate place for this fascinating collection of artifacts, which includes a fine library and archives.

Directions: Near the centre of Halifax, on Gottingen Street, between North and Almon Streets.

Prince of Wales Tower
National Historic Site

Prince Edward—that tireless builder of fortifications, Commander of all Atlantic forces, and the romantic duke of Hemlock Ravine fame—ordered the construction of this massive tower on the highest point of land on Point Pleasant Park. Without approval of the British Parliament, the prince authorized the stone fortification. The North American prototype came to be called a Martello tower.

Captain Straton and his crew built the tower, which was completed in 1796. Round in shape—as were most of the Prince's Halifax buildings—it is the only complete tower remaining of four such forts in the Halifax area (a partial one can be seen at York Redoubt). These forts were intended to protect British sea batteries from a French land attack, and serve as part of the city's coastal defence network. This tower was constructed to serve as an elevated gun platform, a self-defensible battery keep, a barrack, and a storehouse for ammunition and other supplies.

The tower you see today incorporates many alterations made during the period 1796–1865. As you roam through the spartan and cavernous interior you will realize how the tower could hold two hundred men. Even so, its low ceilings can make one feel claustrophobic.

Look for exhibits portraying the tower's history, architectural features, and its significance as a defence structure. Its eight-foot-thick ironstone walls made it impregnable against eighteenth- and nineteenth-century six-pounder guns. Other supplies in the tower would have included 72 muskets, 12 pistols, boarding pikes, and 10,000 ball cartridges. Staff are on hand to answer questions, and interpretive panels guide you through the site. The Prince of Wales National Historic Site is operated by Parks Canada.

Directions: From downtown Halifax take South Park St. to South St. Turn right on South to Tower Road. Turn left on Tower and continue to the Point Pleasant Park carpark at the end of Tower Road. It's a short walk from the carpark, and the trail is signposted.

Prince of Wales Tower: (902) 426-5080 Open: July 1 to Labour Day. The park is open year-round.

The tower is located in the picturesque Point Pleasant Park.

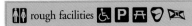 rough facilities

York Redoubt National Historic Site

York Redoubt
National Historic
Site: (902) 426-5080
Open year-round

A redoubt is an independent fortification integrated into a larger defence system. Situated on a high bluff, York Redoubt commands the narrowest part of the entrance to Halifax Harbour, and boasts a stunning panorama. Beginning as a harbour battery in 1793—after France declared war on Great Britain—a small two-gun work was erected at the north end of the present fort. It was enlarged and strengthened by Prince Edward, later the Duke of Kent. He increased the battery of guns and built a stone Martello tower (part of which remains) to replace the old blockhouse.

The biggest structural change was made in the 1860s, with the addition of a more powerful gun called the rifled muzzle loader (RML). The 9-inch gun weighed 12 tonnes, fired 256-pound shells with a range of up to six thousand yards, and required a crew of 9 gunners. These big guns are what you see today when you visit the fort—a state-of-the-art defence system of its time.

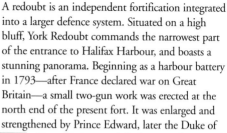

There is much to take in at this site, so bring a picnic and roam or hike at your leisure. There are excellent interpretive panels that explain the ammunition magazine; the landward defence wall behind the guns; the cookhouse and ablution house where the men washed—built in the early 1870s; the engine room—built during World War II; and the fire command post and fortress plotting room used during the Second World War, from where military commanders controlled coastal batteries. You can also see where the anti-submarine net was strung across the harbour from Sleepy Cove below the redoubt to McNabs Island (German U-boats reportedly made it into the outer harbour).

Look down to the dramatic view of the entrance to Halifax Harbour from the site's location, atop a high bluff.

The ruins of a naval barrack and York Shore Battery can be found down by the shore at Sleepy Cove. York Redoubt National Historic Site is operated by Parks Canada.

Directions: By car: approx. 30 mins. from down-town Halifax, on Rte 253 past Purcells Cove. By bus: #15 bus leaves West End Mall once an hour, and leaves the Site once an hour on the hour; on Sundays & holidays at 20 minutes to the hour.

Fort McNab National Historic Site

The significance of Fort McNab, according to historian Don Chard, is that it "represents the evolution of coastal defence technology from the 1880s to the 1940s," which includes advances in ordnance, fire control, and detection. The Mi'kmaq people fished the island waters and hunted in the dense woods. Early Halifax settlers dried their fish catches on the island's beaches. Peter McNab purchased the island in 1782, and much of it stayed in the family for 150 years. In the 1930s his descendants sold off the remaining acres.

The military's use of McNabs Island has been extensive from the 1770s to the end of the Second World War. Among the significant installations were Sherbrooke Tower, Hugonin Battery, Fort Ives and, of course, Fort McNab. Upon landing at Garrison Pier, turn right on Garrison Road. You are heading south, and by keeping to this road you will come to the top of a hill and the entrance to Fort McNab.

The fort was built between 1888 and 1892 to shore up the outer Halifax defences. This was the first fortification in Halifax to use breach-loading guns. In the early 1900s more forceful firepower was introduced, and the fort served as an examination battery in World Wars I and II. Number one and two gun emplacements were modified in 1914 to mount six-inch guns. Upon entering the fort you will notice the remnants of an iron picket fence in the middle of the moat surrounding the fort. There are a number of structures, including the quartermaster's station. There are the outlines of a large bank of bomb-proof casements on site and gun emplacements. Note the radar post constructed in 1945 on top of one of the old gun emplacements. Northwest of that structure sits a pedestal mount with a swivel, which held a ten-inch breach-loading gun, where searchlight emplacements were installed.

Today the island is a natural habitat luring birders, hikers, historians, and picnickers, and is a designated parkland.

Directions: Charter a boat (several to choose from) from Cable Wharf near Halifax's Historic Properties to Garrison Pier on McNabs Island: trip time approx. 30 mins. NOTE: Visiting this site takes the better part of a day. There is no food or drinking water available on the island; and be prepared for changeable weather and for some lengthy walking.

Fort McNab National Historic Site:
(902) 421-8736 for McNabs Island ferry start point & departure times Open year-round, but ferry service is available only during the summer months

1869 Upper Water
Street, Halifax:
(902) 429-0530
Open year-round

"The whole aspect of the town cheerful, thriving and industrious." So wrote Charles Dickens, on an 1842 visit to Halifax. Even a twentieth-century demolition wrecking machine could not dislodge the old ironstone structure of Enos Collins's 1823 warehouse. In the 1960s, Collins' Bank and Warehouse and six other buildings on Privateers'

Wharf were doomed to the land of rubble to make way for Harbour Drive—a proposed waterfront expressway. The buildings were saved—at the last moment—through the dedicated and persistent efforts of the Heritage Trust of Nova Scotia along with faculty members of the Nova Scotia College of Art and Design.

Born in Liverpool, Enos Collins had a strong profile in Halifax. He learned all about business and sea life aboard his father's trading vessels. He began his business in Halifax, and with three ships made a fortune as a privateer raiding American vessels along the New England coastline. He and his partner founded the city's first bank, which was located in Collins' Warehouse.

As you wander around Historic Properties you will come across Collins' Court, Simon's Warehouse, Pickford and Black Building, Privateers' Warehouse, Carpenter Shop, and the Old Red Store. Large, modern second-storey windows open the view to the courts below. These fine stone structures are now occupied by businesses and shops that cater to tourists.

Schooners, marine crafts, and glittering pleasure yachts often moor at the different wharves along the waterfront boardwalk. Along with twenty-one neighbouring nineteenth-century structures on Hollis and Granville Streets, including the 1841 Morse's Tea Building—occupied by the NS College of Art and Design—Historic Properties is one of the finest waterfront attractions in all of Canada.

Stroll along the boardwalk, take in the Victorian architecture and visit the shops.

Directions: On the waterfront, in downtown Halifax.

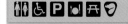

This museum contains the history of Nova Scotia's seafaring past. It was skillfully designed utilizing an authentic shipchandlery and warehouse of the 1870s, with the addition of a contemporary exhibition hall. Prepare to spend at least an hour here, for the collection of marine artifacts is one of the largest in Canada.

Of the six theme galleries, why not begin with the William Robertson and Son Ship chandlery, where in the old days you could buy fishing supplies, a needle, ship's lamps, or an anchor. The smell of tarred rope, barrels, and oilskins hangs in the air. In the Navy room there are ship models, armaments, and artifacts relating to the Royal Canadian Navy. On display in the Shipwrecks and Lifesaving gallery is an authentic old Sable Island lifeboat.

Artifacts from *Titanic* can be found in the second floor Age of Steam gallery. The exhibit, which includes an authentic deckchair and orther memorabilia from the liner that sank off the coast of Newfoundland in April 1912, has been named a top national attraction. Survivors were brought to Halifax, along with many of those who drowned. One hundred and fifty victims of that disaster are buried in Halifax cemeteries.

Not to be missed in the Days of Sail gallery is the recreation of a ship's cabin; sit down and experience the rocking motion and splashing waves.

In the main floor exhibition hall sits Queen Victoria's Royal Barge, in all her glory—over 30 feet long and decorated with gilded dolphins—and permanent exhibits documenting the Halifax Explosion of 1917 and the sinking of *Titanic*. There is also an extensive marine library and visible storage area in the museum. Outside, berthed at the wharf, is the retired Canadian survey vessel, *Acadia*, built in England in 1913. The Maritime Museum of the Atlantic is the marine history branch of the Nova Scotia Museum.

Directions: The Maritime Museum is located on Lower Water Street, on the Halifax waterfront.

Maritime Museum of the Atlantic: 1675 Lower Water St., Halifax (902) 424-7490 or 424-7491; Fax 424-0612 Open year-round June 1-Oct 15: Mon-Sat 9:30 a.m.-5:30 p.m.; Tues to 8 p.m.; Sun 1-5 p.m. Oct 16-May 31: Tues-Sat 9:30 p.m.-5 p.m.; Tues to 8 p.m.; Sun 1-5 p.m. Admission charged June 1–Oct. 15

Marine lovers will find a wealth of fascinating displays and artifacts of the province's nautical history.

Nova Scotia Museum of Natural History

Nova Scotia Museum
of Natural History:
1747 Summer Street,
Halifax (902) 424-
7353; recorded info:
424-6099
Open year-round
June 1-Oct 15: Mon-
Sat 9:30 a.m.-5:30
p.m.; Wed to 8 p.m.;
Sun 1-5 p.m.
Oct 16-May 31: Tues-
Sat 9:30 a.m.-5 p.m.;
Wed to 8 p.m.; Sun 1-
5 p.m.

Birds, bats, nests,
bones, walrus tusks
and freshwater
sponges are all
found in the
museum's displays.

This fine museum, with its changing displays, is a place for hands-on activities, especially for youngsters. You may even be greeted in the foyer by a loveable old relic, Gus the tortoise.

The museum's focus is on the natural history of Nova Scotia. Natural wonders can be discovered through exhibitions, displays, and activities such as a live, in-house bee colony, shore-life aquariums and the summer Butterfly House with real butterflies.

One of the unique features of the museum is the archaeological showroom. Here you learn about the history of the Mi'kmaq from prehistoric days to contact with European settlers. The Mi'kmaq have played an important part in the development of Nova Scotia. Without their help, early settlers could not have survived the harsh conditions they faced in Nova Scotia. Chief Membertou was always a welcome guest at Champlain's Order of Good Cheer banquets—celebrations that helped pass the harsh Nova Scotian winters—at the Port Royal Habitation in the early 1600s. And the Mi'kmaq helped the Acadians when they were attacked by

English soldiers. The display of the Mi'kmaq way of life and artifacts covers more than 10,600 years of settlement by First Nation People in what we know as Nova Scotia.

Also not to be missed is the Rare for a Reason display, addressing extinct and endangered species of Nova Scotia.

Look for the geological gallery, which has fossil specimens including a mastodon bone unearthed in 1835. In the marine gallery is an enormous skeleton of a pilot whale. There are sea bird dioramas, insectivores, and a display of Nova Scotia gold, the latter found in the geology gallery.

Directions: The museum is on Summer Street, a short walk from the Public Gardens and Spring Garden Road in the centre of Halifax. Admission charged June 1–Oct 15.

 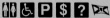

Province House
National Historic Site

In comparison with other provincial legislative buildings, Province House may seem rather small. However, it is one of the finest examples of Palladian style architecture in North America. Opened in 1819, the building's exterior was restored in 1985–87 by professional stonemasons from England, who worked with 12 local apprentices.

This is a beautifully proportioned building, classic in design with a charming interior. Someone once wrote that "more history has been made inside Province House than in all other nine provincial legislative buildings combined." Examples include the birth of responsible government in the British Commonwealth, establishment of freedom of the press, and free school legislation. Province House is also home to the first legislative assembly in Canada.

The Georgian interior is intricate and highly ornamental. The tall windows in the Red Chamber are decoratively outlined with motifs of acorns, roses, lions' heads and thistles. In the mezzanine there is a grand staircase flanked by Ionic columns.

On the grounds at the southern end of Province House you can see a fine statue of Joseph Howe, one of the most renowned Nova Scotian statesmen of the last century. Howe, owner of the influential newspaper, *The Novascotian*, was an elected member of the legislature, and later served as Premier of the province. Province House is the seat of the Nova Scotia Government, Canada's oldest provincial legislative assembly, and the home of Britain's first overseas self-government.

Directions: Front entrance of the site is located in downtown Halifax on Granville Street, bounded by Prince, Granville, and George Streets.

1726 Hollis Street, Halifax (902) 424-4661
Open year-round
July-Aug: Mon-Fri
9 a.m.-5 p.m.;
Sat & Sun & holidays
10 a.m.-4 p.m.
Off season: Mon-Fri
9 a.m.-4 p.m.

Joseph Howe served as Speaker of the House, Premier of the province, and was a for a short time the Lieutenant-Governor.

Our Lady of Sorrows Chapel

Holy Cross Cemetery,
Halifax
Open Apr-Oct: Mon-
Fri 8:30 a.m.-4:30 p.m.

The most remarkable fact about this little chapel is
that it was built in one day. On August 31, 1843,
over 1,800 people gathered to construct this charming house of worship. The fragments of French

stained glass windows
date to the sixteenth
and seventeenth cen-
turies, and there are
replica wooden carvings
from a Flemish church
of the 1550s.

Sir John Thompson
Prime Minister of
Canada (1892–1894)
is buried in Holy
Cross Cemetery.

Directions: Located in
Holy Cross Cemetery,
South Park & Morris
Streets, South End
Halifax.

64

Little Dutch Church

Little Dutch Church:
(902) 425-3658;
Fax 422-9446
Church service 4 pm
Sunday. Available for
viewing 9 am to 5 pm
weekdays mid-May
to Aug.

This quaint and tiny house of worship began as a
humble log cabin fashioned by Evangelical
Lutherans. About two dozen German families
chose to settle in Halifax shortly after the city was
founded in 1749, while thousands of other German
and European colonists settled along the South
Shore in the Lunenburg area.

Master carpenter Christopher Cleesattel turned
the log structure into the building you see today.
The church measures only 40 by 20 feet (12 by 6
metres). It was moved to its present location in
1756 and served as Saint George's Church until the
parishioners built the Round Church in 1800. It
was subsequently used as a school.

A wall tablet tells us that
a Reverend Bernard M.
Houseal, from Wurtenburg,
Germany, was pastor from
1785 to 1799 and lies
interred beneath the church.
Because the German settlers
called themselves "Deutsch,"
this first Lutheran church in
Canada became known as "The Little Dutch
Church."

This small church is
a legacy of the
German families who
settled in Halifax in
the 18th century.

Directions: From downtown Halifax, follow
Brunswick Street north; Little Dutch Church is on
Brunswick at Gerrish Street.

Saint George's Round Church

Saint George's—a beloved Anglican church—has often been called an "architectural gem." It was built in 1800 to accommodate the growing congregation of the Little Dutch Church, just a block away. This is Canada's only round church—there are only five round churches left in England—and it seems fitting that Prince Edward, later Duke of Kent, influenced its design. It is a superb example of the late eighteenth-century revival of interest in the classical forms adopted by Inigo Jones.

Saint George's began as a perfect circle. The original church was basically a large cylinder with a smaller one on top supporting a dome. The cupola, housing a bell, topped this structure. A chancel, organ loft and porch, and vestry were added later, yet the building has retained its fine classical lines. In 1835 Halley's comet flared across the sky, inspiring the church's rector to have a comet-shaped weathervane mounted on the cupola.

Inside, twelve wooden pillars support the main balcony, and rising above that are two more balconies. However, the uppermost balcony is hidden behind arches at the base of the domed ceiling. Long ago, slaves and servants were squeezed into this small area to sit on bone-hard benches. On the main floor are steps leading up to the altar. To the left of the altar a wall plaque tells us that one of the longest-serving rectors of this parish—45 years—was the beloved and revered Robert Fitzgerald Uniacke, MA (1791-1870). High-backed pews run along the curve of the church wall. The domed ceiling rises high above the stacked galleries.

A third of the structure, including the dome, was lost in a fire in June 1994. The generosity of Nova Scotians and people across Canada has made it possible to restore the church to its former glory. This has always been a well-attended church and the parish reaches out to the community in many ways. Saint George's is a National Historic Site.

Directions:

From downtown Halifax, follow Brunswick Street north; Saint George's is located on Brunswick Street at Cornwallis. It is within a block of the Little Dutch Church.

Saint George's Round Church:
(902) 425-3658;
Fax 422-9446
Main Sunday service 10:30 a.m., all welcome.
Available for viewing 9 am to 5 pm weekdays mid-May to Aug.

Saint George's Round Church balcony (above) and exterior (below).

St. Paul's Anglican
Church:
1749 Argyle Street,
Halifax (902) 429-2240
Open year-round:
Mon-Fri 9 a.m.-
4:30 p.m.
Summer:
Mon-Sat 9 a.m.-5 p.m.
Sunday services
year-round: 8 a.m.-
9:15 a.m.; 11 a.m.

"Thus came into existence the mother temple of the Church of England in Canada," wrote Thomas Raddall of St. Paul's Anglican Church. The doors to St. Paul's Anglican Church opened on September 2, 1750, and the church became the first public building in the new town of Halifax. It was the first garrison church in Halifax and is the oldest Protestant church in Canada.

This glorious wooden house of worship sits overlooking the site of the old garrison parade grounds in the heart of downtown Halifax. The architectural plans of St. Paul's were based on those made by James Gibbs of St. Peter's Church in London, England; Gibbs was a pupil of Sir Christopher Wren. The oak frame and pine timbers were shipped from Boston, and thousands of local bricks were used for infill to line the walls. The original structure remains as sound today as it was those few centuries ago.

Inside, the stained glass windows—one of which dates back to 1868—depict the crucifixion, resurrection, and ascension of Christ. Look for the "explosion window" on the west wall of the upper level. The original window was broken by the force of the blast that blew up the *Mont Blanc*, and levelled much of Halifax in 1917. The window is famous because despite the replacement of new glass, there remains the ghostly silhouette of a head and shoulders—reputedly the image of a man thrown through the window during the explosion.

St. Paul's is the oldest Protestant church in Canada.

You will also find the Royal Pew, reserved for the queen, or her representative—the Lieutenant-Governor— and the dozens of memorial tablets that form a fascinating record of those who have occupied St. Paul's pews over the centuries.

Under the floor are twenty burial vaults of early worshippers at St. Paul's. In the narthex you will find a list of the illustrious dead in the Memorial Book. This impressive and dignified church still serves worshippers today.

Directions: **Downtown Halifax, between Barrington and Argyle Streets, at the Grand Parade square.**

Lighthouse Route

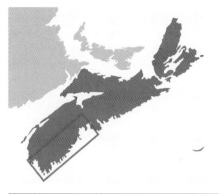

Lighthouse Trail

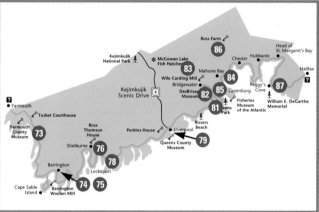

73. Argyle Township Court House & Gaol
74. Barrington Woolen Mill Museum
75. The Old Meeting House Museum
76. Dory Shop Museum
77. Ross-Thomson House and Store Museum
78. Lockeport First Provincially Registered Streetscape & Little School Museum
79. Perkins House Museum
80. Queens County Museum

81. Fort Point Museum
82. DesBrisay Museum & National Exhibition Centre
83. Wile Carding Mill Museum
84. Mahone Bay Settlers Museum
85. Fisheries Museum of the Atlantic, St. John's Anglican Church & Lunenburg Academy National Historic Site
86 Ross Farm Museum
87 Village of Peggys Cove & deGarthe Memorial

Introduction

The Lighthouse Route wends its way along Nova Scotia's South Shore from Halifax to Yarmouth past bays and inlets dotted with tiny islands—remnants of the last Ice Age. The coastline is filled with legends of intrigue and piracy. Did Captain Kidd leave his ill-gotten treasure on Mahone Bay's Oak Island, or is it the Holy Grail that lies in the fabled money pit, hidden there by Prince Henry Sinclair, a Knight Templar, who is said to have visited in 1398. We do know that rum-runners kept their illicit stills hidden there from the eyes of Canadian inspectors during Prohibition.

The history of this area is largely the history of seafaring. Deep-sea trawlers pull into Lunenburg Harbour where the famed *Bluenose* was built and

from where she first set sail. Widow's walks abound atop seafront houses—a reminder of those women who awaited the safe return of their sailor husbands and sons. It is no wonder that it is called the Lighthouse Route. The lights remain, but not the keepers. All Nova Scotia lights are now automated.

Visitors can find sites of rich historical interest along the shoreline roads of the Lighthouse Route.

The Mi'kmaq were here first. The natural bays were ideal for summer fishing camps. Later Champlain mapped the area from Yarmouth to LaHave. Descendants of the Acadians who followed after him still live in the Pubnico region.

The South Shore has always had close ties with the New England States. After the American Revolution, United Empire Loyalists came in the hundreds for the promised land grants in British North America. Among them were a substantial number of Black Loyalists, many of whom settled in the Shelburne area. In the ensuing years there have been immigrants from all parts of Europe, including English, Scots, Irish, Germans, Dutch, and Scandinavians. They farmed, fished, or built boats. They erected homes, schools, and churches, and established small businesses in their communities.

Argyle Township Court House & Gaol

In pioneering Nova Scotia, structures such as forts and churches had building priority. Strangely enough, legal proceedings had to be held in taverns, rented rooms, or in general stores. Eventually the need for courthouses became critical. In October 1805 the first Court of General Sessions was held in the Argyle Township Court House and Gaol at Tusket, Nova Scotia. This building has survived intact and today is acknowledge as the oldest standing courthouse in Canada.

Argyle Township
Court House & Gaol:
(902) 648-2493
Open June 1-30:
Mon-Fri 9 a.m.-5 p.m.
July 1-Aug 30: Daily
9 a.m.-5 p.m.

The ground-floor entrance leads into a cool, damp cell corridor. The double cell for debtors originally had one window with twelve panes, while the single cells had six paned windows with bars. Various jail breaks over the years resulted in the installation of new security measures. In the 1870s the cell windows were removed. The cell doors are solid steel with a small grill. Even on the brightest day there is not enough light to read a book in these cells.

The small, scantily furnished room containing such basics as a cot and washstand was the jailer's quarters. On the wall hangs a pair of nineteenth-century handcuffs, a billy club, and a large ring of keys. The spiral staircase in the front vestibule leads to the second floor of the courthouse and courtroom.

From the judge's podium, you can see the Tusket River from almost every window in the room.

On each side of the courtroom are the jury benches. The clerk's table is positioned in front of the judge's podium, next to a rack for drying documents from the era of the quill pen.

Above the jail cells is the courtroom (above) where the prisoners would go to wait for sentencing.

The Court of General Sessions was held once a year from 1805 onward. Supreme Court sat here for the first time in 1836 and continued on an annual basis until 1925. That same year the jail was closed as well. Magistrates' Court convened here on a regular basis from 1925 until 1945 when the building ceased to function as a working courthouse.

Directions: From Highway 103, take Exit 33 to 8168 Highway 3 in Tusket.

Lighthouse
Trail

Barrington Woolen Mill Museum

Barrington Woolen
Mill Museum:
(902) 637-2185
Open June 15-
Sept 30:
Mon-Sat 9:30 a.m.-
5:30 p.m.;
Sun 1-5:30 p.m.

Not far from the Old Meeting House in Barrington, the road takes a curve and there, in a pastoral
setting of trees, flowing river, rocks, and a foot-
bridge, is the Woolen Mill. Inside the two-storey
mill, built in 1882, eight men and women spent
eleven-hour workdays under dim lighting and the
constant hum and racket of mechanized looms.
Strict rules forbade employees talking to each other
without permission.

The woolen mill made life easier for women.
Long before the mill was built, men sheared the
sheep while almost everything else was accomplished by women's hands: washing the wool, picking, carding, spinning, dyeing, and knitting.

The hum and racket is still present as you are
taken through the milling process by interpreters.
Powered by a water turbine, the mill carding and
spinning machines churned out miles of yarns to

make blankets and cloth
goods. The first two
decades of the twentieth
century saw the mill's peak
production. It then
declined steadily until
World War II brought
heavy demands for yarns,
and the mill was busy once
again until it closed forever

The mill stayed in
operation until 1962
when competition
and a commercial
influx of cheaper
materials forced its
closure.

in 1962. The mill is the last of many small woolen
factories that were built across Nova Scotia during
the latter part of the nineteenth century.

The mill museum
remains just as it
was in 1882.

Directions: From Highway 103, follow old Route 3
from Shelburne to Barrington.

The Old Meeting House Museum

Four years after they first began arriving in Barrington, Nova Scotia, God-fearing New England settlers began plans to erect a meeting house. In November, 1767 the first worship service was held.

All "Preachers of the Gospel" were welcome; Baptists, Methodists, and Presbyterians delivered long and severe sermons. Consistent with the Puritan belief "that a person's religion lacked fire if it could not provide enough warmth throughout a service," there was no heating so worshippers brought wrapped hot stones (or their family dog) to keep their feet warm. Each wooden pew row was equipped with a buttoned door to keep out draughts.

(902) 637-2185
Open June 15-Sept 30: Mon-Sat 9:30 a.m.-5:30 p.m.; Sun 1-5:30 p.m.

The Old Meeting House, built in 1761, is the only structure of its kind in Nova Scotia.

Heavy oak timbers, probably from nearby Sherose Island, frames the structure, with trunnels (treenails) fastening the hand-hewn beams. The wide floorboards were probably brought from New England, since Barrington was incapable of sawing such large planks at the time. Natural growth knees, similar to those used by boat builders, strengthened the wall beams.

The upstairs balcony houses "overflow" pews. The balcony panels and wall pulpit with its stairs and swinging door were added in the 1780s. Natural light shines through the 352 small window panes, some of which are original.

Also used as a civic meeting place for events such as town meetings and elections, the oldest non-conformist house of worship in Canada is still used each Christmas for carol singing, accompanied by the old American-made organ. All are welcome to attend the community service held annually on the third Sunday in August.

Directions: Follow Highway 103 or old Route 3 from Shelburne. The museum is across the bridge from the Mill Museum in Barrington.

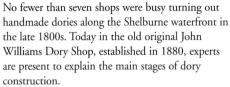
Dory Shop Museum:
(902) 875-3219
Open June 1-Sept 30:
Daily 9:30 a.m.-5:30
p.m.

No fewer than seven shops were busy turning out handmade dories along the Shelburne waterfront in the late 1800s. Today in the old original John Williams Dory Shop, established in 1880, experts are present to explain the main stages of dory construction.

When you enter the shop there is the scent of hardwood and pine, dory paint, and fresh wood shavings. You may even witness the building of a

dory. A dory is easy to admire, with its curved or bowed lines from stem to transom. At one time it was the most popular small craft in the Atlantic Provinces, used in off-shore schooner fishing, particularly on the Newfoundland Grand Banks. Holding two men and laden with fishing gear and bait, the dory was ideal for both hand-lining and trawl fishing. Light-weight and sturdy, the flat-bottomed boats could be hoisted and lowered from a schooner, often full of fish, and then nested one on top of the other on the deck.

Here you can have an up-close look at the dories or even the chance to sit inside of one.

Dory fishing declined in the 1940s, but the Williams shop stayed in business until 1971. The shop was officially reopened in 1983 as part of the Nova Scotia Museum family by Their Royal Highnesses, the Prince and Princess of Wales. Craftsmen continue the fine tradition of creating these unique boats.

Directions: Exit 25 from 103 on to Route 3; down-town Shelburne waterfront.

♿ partial **P** **?** ⛴

Ross-Thomson House & Store

This is the only surviving eighteenth-century store in Nova Scotia. Look for a large two-storey building on Charlotte Lane near Dock Street in Shelburne. The wooden New England-style structure rests on a granite foundation, has a gambrel roof, thick planked doors, and birchbark-trimmed windows.

Loyalists sailed here from America in 1783. They founded the town and called it Port Roseway, which was later renamed Shelburne by Governor John Parr. Shelburne's population soon burgeoned to 10,000 inhabitants to become one of the largest towns in North America at the time. Among those who landed were 2,000 Black African freed slaves, many of whom had fought for the British during the Revolutionary War; they established an enduring presence in Shelburne and other communities all along the coast.

George and Robert Ross, brothers from Scotland, conducted their business from this historic building. Trade was brisk: codfish, spars, pickled herring, and pine planks were exchanged for such things as sugar, molasses, and rum from the West Indies, wine from Madeira, tobacco from the southern states, and flour from New England. By 1809 business had waned, and within twenty years the boomtown was reduced to a population of 300. The store passed into the Thomson family and in the 1880s it was closed.

Inside, in the east end of the building, look for Robert Thomson's desk, still standing in the corner beside the fireplace. Notice the wooden barrels lining the floor, and coils of rope in front of a counter wide enough to spread, measure, and cut fabrics. On the shelves are blankets, spools of thread, pots, and fine china from England. The south end of the building was used for living quarters

Directions: Take Exit 25 from Highway 103 on to Route 3; the museum is along the downtown Shelburne waterfront, on Charlotte Lane.

Ross-Thomson House & Store: (902) 875-3219 Open June 1-Oct 15: Daily 9:30 a.m.- 5:30 p.m.

Ross Thomson House reflects Loyalist lifestyle after the American revolution.

Lockeport: 1st Provincially Registered Streetscape & Little School Museum

School Museum:
(902) 656-2989 or
(902) 656-2910
Open July -Labour
Day: Mon-Sat
10 a.m.-4 p.m.

The Locke homestead, built in 1876.

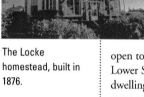

Locke family streetscape memorial.

The mile-long sandy Crescent Beach—immortalized on a former $50 Canadian bill—was a busy tourist attraction in Lockeport at the turn of the century. The harbour was crowded with billowing sails as schooners carried out a booming West Indies trade. This thriving fishing village was settled by New England Planters around 1760-61, and among the first to arrive were Josiah Churchill and Jonathan Locke, MD.

The five Locke family houses on Lower South Street reflect the town's illustrious past with Colonial, Georgian, and Victorian architecture. The only house of the five open to the public is on the corner of John and Lower South Streets. This Second Empire-style dwelling was built by Captain Locke in 1876. The most striking room is the Victorian parlour: on its walls hang the original dark floral Victorian paper, elegantly highlighted with gold. The ceilings are decorated using geometric lines of different shades, creating the illusion of a fresco. Helen Ghent and her son, descendants of Captain Locke, care for the Victorian furnishings and antiques that give the house its air of dignity and richness.

As you stroll along the street, note the oldest standing structure in Lockeport, a rare example of Georgian-style architecture in Nova Scotia. Another place of interest is the Little School Museum, purchased by the Garden Club in 1967 through donations from former students. The building was used as a school from 1845 until it was turned into a dwelling. Today the various rooms hold artifacts, with one furnished as a nineteenth-century village schoolroom with desks, slates, copy books, inkwells, and straight pens.

Directions: Take Exit 23, off Route 105, follow old route to Lockeport. The five Locke family houses that make up the historic streetscape are situated on Lower South Street, near the waterfront. The Little School Museum is at 29 & 37 Locke Street.

School Museum: 🚻 🅿

Perkins House Museum

Personages from royal governors to wandering preachers have found themselves both welcomed and entertained in the one-and-a-half-storey Cape Cod-style home, whose doors remain open to this day for anyone interested in examining the life of Simeon Perkins.

Perkins was one of many New England Planters who settled in Nova Scotia in the 1760s. He arrived in Liverpool from Connecticut in 1762 and built his home in 1766 to accommodate his ever-expanding family, which included his second wife Elizabeth, ten children, and three servants. The house is composed of nine period-furnished rooms, including the back parlour Perkins used as his study.

Perkins House:
(902) 354-4058
Open June 1-Oct 15:
Mon-Sat. 9:30 a.m.-
5:30 p.m; Sun 1- 5:30
p.m.

It was in his parlour that—despite sometimes freezing temperatures—Perkins vigilantly kept a diary of Liverpool comings and goings, as well as of his own life for forty-six years. He made note of everything from weather reports, movements of settlers, births, deaths, marriages, and shipping news. His diaries tell us how the American Revolution put him and other settlers in a difficult and painful situation, as they found themselves fighting in retaliation against their American countrymen during attacks along the Nova Scotia shoreline.

Perkins House Museum (top); Simeon Perkins (above)

Holding many town positions, including Colonel of the Queens County militia and Justice of the Court of Common Pleas, Simeon Perkins—diarist, businessman, and ship owner—was never bored. He died in 1812 at the age of 78, having recorded some of the most detailed accounts of Liverpool in tumultuous and exciting British North America.

Directions: From Highway 103, take Exit 19 to Liverpool. Perkins House Museum is located at 105 Main Street, Liverpool, a few blocks from the downtown area.

Perkins and his wife raised their ten children in this house.

Queens County
Museum:
(902) 354-4058
Open year-round
June 1-Oct 15: Mon-
Sat 9:30 a.m.-5:30
p.m.; Sun 1-5:30 p.m.
Oct 16-May 31: Mon-
Sat 9 a.m.-5 p.m.

The museum has a
quilt exhibit.

Liverpool was home to Thomas Raddall, a twentieth-century writer and historian who won awards
for his superb novels and non-fiction works. It was
Raddall who, as president of Queens County
Historical Society, helped to lay the groundwork
for the purchase of the Perkins house in 1949. In
his own diary, Raddall kept a daily record of the
restoration of the building.

The museum attractions include the Thomas
Raddall Room, a re-creation of Raddall's study with
original furnishings that belonged to the writer.
There are permanent exhibits relating to forestry,
Mi'kmaq life, privateering, shipbuilding, and a
working model railroad representing the county rail
lines.

Directions: The Queens County Museum is located
next door to Perkins House Museum, at 109 Main
Street, Liverpool.

81 ## Fort Point Museum

Fort Point Museum
(902) 688-2696 Open
June-Aug: 10 a.m.-
5:30 p.m. Weekend in
Sept: 1-5 p.m.

The river, the 100-foot (30.5-metre) bluffs of Cape
LaHave, the islands at the river's mouth, the bay,
and the village of Petite Riviere are as captivating
now as the day in 1604 when Champlain inked it
all on his map.

For a short time, even before Port Royal, Fort
Point was the capital of New France in Acadia.
What you see today is the site of the French fort
and permanent settlement established in 1632 by
Isaac de Razilly, a distinguished naval officer and
Knight Commander of the Order of St. John of
Jerusalem (Order of Malta). The settlement included a chapel for the three Capuchin monks who
first brought education to New France and provided instruction for the Mi'kmaq as well as other
colonists. Today the location includes a lighthouse
that also serves as a museum.

Directions: Travelling on Highway 103, take
Exit 12, follow Route 331 to LaHave. Fort Point is
located at 100 Fort Point Road in La Have.

Queens Museum:	
Ft. Point Museum:	

DesBrisay Museum & National Exhibition Centre

DesBrisay Museum in Bridgewater is Nova Scotia's oldest municipal museum and a fine educational institute. It is set on 25 acres (10 hectares) of parkland filled with protected woodlands, nature trails, a bird sanctuary, and a natural pond.

The museum's permanent exhibits tell the story of Lunenburg County and the people who settled in the area. The Mi'kmaq, French, English, and Germans are represented by the tools and implements they once used. Look for the quillwork on an 1841 Mi'kmaq cradle.

DesBrisay Museum: (902) 543-4033
Open year-round
May 15-Sept 30: Mon-Sat 9 a.m.-5 p.m.; Sun 1-5 p.m.
Oct 1-May 1: Tues-Sun 1-5 p.m.; Wed to 9 p.m.

Once you've taken in the museum's displays, stroll through the neighbouring parkland.

The museum is named in honour of Mather Byles DesBrisay—historian, county judge, and avid collector of curious objects. His book, *History of the County of Lunenburg*, written in 1895, preserves for us the memories, events, and ways of life in the area during the last century. The DesBrisay Museum had its origins in a private collection established in the 1880s by the judge. In 1965 the collection was given its present permanent home. In 1974 a new wing was added to display major travelling exhibits from across Canada.

An agriculture exhibit is a popular feature at the DesBrisay Museum.

Directions: From Route 103 take Exit 12 to Bridgewater, and proceed across the bridge; turn left on King Street and then right on Jubilee Road. The museum is at 130 Jubilee Road.

Lighthouse Trail

Wile Carding Mill:
(902) 543-8233
Open June 1-Sept 30:
Mon-Sat 9:30 a.m.-
5:30 p.m.; Sun 1-5:30
p.m.

When Dean Wile built his wool carding mill in 1860, the meadows of Lunenburg County were filled with 16,786 sheep. No wonder that during peak shearing season the mill operated twenty-four hours a day, six days a week to keep up with the demand. Located on a brook, the mill shared water power with a couple of sawmills and grist mills, a foundry, a carriage factory, and a tannery.

Today the red painted mill sits near a millpond that attracts ducks, muskrats, and curious visitors.

The picturesque Wile Carding Museum.

Inside the dimly lit shed, an interpreter points out the bulky machines for picking, carding, and batting wool. The batts were used as quilt fillings, and finished cardings, called rolays, were taken home to be spun on a wheel and the yarn used to knit socks and sweaters.

The noisy picking machine operated in a separate room because it spewed out oil and wool. The interpreter will open the sluice gates to let the brook water rush through. When the power is on listen for the bumping sound of the water wheel.

Wile's grandson, Vernon, inherited the mill in 1936 and ran it as a part-time business until 1968. The Wile Carding Mill became part of the Nova Scotia Museum family in 1974, and is managed by the nearby DesBrisay Museum.

When the mill opened in 1860, it was run by three women who were paid two dollars for their seventy-two hour work weeks.

Directions: From Highway 103, take Exit 11. Follow Route 325 to Pearl Street and Victoria Road in Bridgewater. The museum is at 242 Victoria Rd.

Mahone Bay Settlers Museum

The approach to the village of Mahone Bay can be breathtaking and unforgettable: clouds drift over the bay; sailboat masts shine in the afternoon sun; and the three famous churches perch in a row, their tall spires reflecting in the water. This beguiling setting attracts not only visitors, but filmmakers.

The museum is housed in the Benjamin Begin House (c.1850). Highly visible is the distinctive "Lunenburg bump," a two-storey front porch indigenous to Lunenburg County. Benjamin was a sailmaker, and models and tools are on display in the sail loft. There are interpretive displays about the settlement of the area by foreign Protestants in 1754, hand-painted china (c. 1890–30) by local artist Alice Hagene, as well as an important collection of ceramics from Lunenburg County. The interior of the house is furnished in period style.

Mahone Bay Settlers Museum (902) 624-6263
Open mid-May-Sept 30: Tues-Fri 10 a.m. - 5 p.m.; Sat 1-5 p.m.

Directions: From Highway 103, take Exit 10 to 578 Main St., Mahone Bay.

Include a visit to the Settlers Museum in your visit to Mahone Bay.

Lighthouse Trail

Fisheries Museum of the Atlantic; St. John's Anglican Church; Lunenburg Academy National Histoirc Site

Fisheries Museum of the Atlantic

Fisheries Museum of the Atlantic:
(902) 634-4794
Open May 22-Oct 15:
Daily 9:30 a.m.-
5:30 p.m.
Off season: Mon-Fri
8:30 a.m.-4:30 p.m.
Admission charged
during the season.

Located on the waterfront in Lunenburg's "Old Town" section—a UNESCO World Heritage Site—the museum depicts the significance of the sea in the lives of Nova Scotians. The wharfside museum consists of buildings and vessels that commemorate the East Coast fishing tradition. You are encouraged to visit famous deep-sea fishing vessels and talk with fishermen about the days on the

Grand Banks. You may see a boat being built, a lobster trap being made, or fish being filleted. Be sure to visit the three floors of exhibits. There is also an aquarium, a theatre, and a short history of the schooner *Bluenose* .

Here you will find the largest collection in the region devoted to the fishery industry.

Directions: From Route 103, take Exit 11 and proceed to downtown Lunenburg.

St. John's Anglican Church

St. John's Anglican Church:
(902)634-4994
Open summer months: Sunday services.

With its lavish architecture and neo-Gothic pinnacles rising skywards, it is hard to believe that St. John's Anglican Church began as a humble meeting house in 1753. Painted white with black trim, St. John's is one of the oldest Anglican churches in Canada, second only to St. Paul's in Halifax. The

original parish register has entries dating as far back as 1783 recording births, deaths, and marriages. Founded by royal charter, the church retains communion vessels presented by King George III and a Queen Anne pewter chalice.

The present church, built in 1874, summons followers with its 70-foot (21-metre) tower that holds 8,000 pounds (3,654 kg) of cast-iron hung bells, carefully tested for just the right tones. The oak frame was shipped from Boston before local mills were established. But the sanctuary's hammerbeam ceiling is native pine, lending a Gothic-style accent to the church's warm and friendly interior of dark

St. John's striking exterior design.

Discover Nova Scotia Historic Sites

Museum: 🚻 ♿ 🅿 🛏 💲 ❓ ⛴

wooden pews, wooden floor, and marble pillars. Sermons were sometimes delivered to packed galleries in English, German, and French from the lectern, where a 1783 edition of the Book of Common Prayer sits, guarded by a brass eagle.

Try to visit this "Carpenter Gothic" building on a bright day, and notice how the light flows through the exquisite stained glass into the chancel.

Directions: From Route 103, take Exit 11 and head for Lunenburg. The church is located on Cumberland Street, at Cornwallis in Lunenburg.

Lunenburg Academy Provincial Historic Site

Sitting high above the town on Gallows Hill is Lunenburg Academy. On September 28, 1893, the original one-storey, four-classroom building "caught fire and burned to ashes, no lives lost ... cause of fire a defective flue," wrote J. Moyle Rudolph. It was replaced in 1895 by the "Castle on the Hill," as it is sometimes called.

New Brunswick architect Harry H. Mott spent every day carefully overseeing the construction of the new building from start to finish. It's an elaborate building, three storeys high with a 600-pound (272-kg) bell in the front tower, an assembly hall, library, laboratory, and twelve classrooms. Inside, the roomy classrooms fill with natural light through large windows. The ceilings are wood-panelled, and birch wainscoting lines the classrooms and halls.

Lovers of old buildings won't soon forget this palatial, traditional-style building. It has a mansard roof, Queen Anne-style asymmetrical towers, oval and Palladian-style dormer windows, triangular pediments, and horizontal banding.

Now an official National Historic Site, the school once taught all grades but today is for elementary students only. The building stands as a fine tribute to its architect, and a reminder of a less hectic era, when pride was taken in craftsmanship.

Directions: Lunenburg Academy is situated on Gallows Hill, Lunenburg.

Lunenburg Academy Provincial Historic Site (902)634-1895 FAX (902) 634-7194 Currently under restoration, regularly scheduled weekly tours of the school will resume in summer 2000.

Tours of the Lunenburg Academy can be arranged during the summer and for special events.

Ross Farm Museum,
New Ross (902) 689-
2210; Fax 689-2264
Open June 1-Oct 15:
Daily 9:30 a.m.-5:30
p.m.
Jan 2-March 17: Sat
and Sun only 9:30
a.m.-4:30 p.m.
Admission charged.

Rural life in nineteenth-century Nova Scotia is vividly depicted at Ross Farm Museum. In 1816 Captain John Ross and 172 disbanded British soldiers were given government land grants to begin a settlement at Sherbrooke, later called New Ross. Ross cleared 56 of his 800 acres to build his farm. After being stationed halfway around the world as a soldier, he settled here with his wife Mary and four children. The farm has been worked by five generations of the Ross family.

Today descendants of the early settlers take part in demonstrating the skills and techniques of the nineteenth-century craftsmen: the blacksmith working at his forge, striking sparks on the anvil to change the shape of a piece of hot iron; and the cooper using curve-shaped staves of local softwood and banding them with hoops to make a barrel.

Enjoy the museum's many live workshops.

Roam around the old barn with its farm animals representing many rarer heritage breeds and visit the second-floor displays of early ploughs and farm machinery. The farm workshop is a delight for youngsters, who can watch butter being churned and wooden toys being made. The old general store is stocked much as it was in the nineteenth century, with patent medicines, fabrics, tools, dishes, pots, and pans. Do not miss the wonderful collection of nineteenth-century horse-drawn wagons, carts, and sleighs in the lower barn. You might even see oxen or horses pulling a hay rake or a plough.

The 1817 Rose Bank Cottage kitchen, constructed with hand-hewn logs, was the heart and soul of social life at the farm. At the Peddler's Shop

The farm's sleigh rides are a lively reminder of a bygone age.

you can buy produce and handmade articles from the farm kitchen.

Directions: Follow Route 12 to the South Shore (Exit 9), 15 mi. from Chester Basin to New Ross.

Village of Peggys Cove & William E. deGarthe Memorial Provincial Park

Snug and salty Peggys Cove has been photographed, painted, and written about countless times, but the wild and rocky views from this tranquil fishing village never grow old. Once upon a time children opened and closed the village gate to keep roving cattle and oxen out of the gardens. Thousands of tourists now navigate the twisting road into the preservation area each year.

Once there, take some time to visit the Fishermen's Monument. The granite wall carvings by Finnish-born William E. deGarthe depict working fishermen led by the legendary Peggy. Next to the monument is the deGarthe Gallery, which carries a display of his seascape and ship paintings inspired by his love for the landscape and ocean view of the windswept cove.

Peggys Cove: (902) 823-1074 William E. de Garthe Memorial Provincial Park open year-round

And, of course, no visit to Peggys Cove would be complete without taking a stroll around its famous lighthouse and rugged rocks. The first lighthouse was built in 1868 to help vessels of all kinds navigate safely into St. Margarets Bay channel. It was simply a house with a blinking light on top. The present structure, standing since 1914, serves as a summer post office—a Canadian one-of-a-kind.

William deGarthe was 70 when he began sculpting the 100-ft long Fishermen's Monument (below).

The folds of granite, shale, and sandstone metamorphosed into slate and quartzite—a geologist's dream—are perfect for a windy walk. The rock pools, granite ledges, and small "canyons" provide excellent places for children to play. But be warned: raging winds and rogue waves come up unexpectedly, and have carried several unsuspecting tourists off the slippery rocks and out to sea.

Directions: From Highway 103, follow Route 333 to Peggys Cove.

Index